Rightsizing

A SMART Living 365 Guide To

Reinventing Retirement

Kathy Gottberg

Rightsizing

A SMART Living 365 Guide to

Reinventing Retirement

Copyright © 2016 by Kathy Gottberg

Cover Design and Illustration by: Thom Gottberg

ISBN-13: 978-1517467029

ISBN-10: 1517467020

ALSO BY KATHY GOTTBERG:

BOOKS

The FINDHORN Book of
Practical Spirituality

The Complete Guide to Selling Your Own Home
In California

Finding Grace
A Transformational Journey

Simple * SMART & Happy
A SMART Living Guide
To A Sustainable & Meaningful Lifestyle

WEBSITES

SMART Living 365.com

KathyGottberg.com

ACKNOWLEDGMENTS

I am incredibly grateful to be surrounded by an enormous number of kind, generous and awesome people in my life. Nothing I've ever done or written was done alone. Most of all, I am overwhelmingly thankful for my husband Thom who is my biggest fan and muse.

I also owe a debt of gratitude to three "Accountability Partners" who helped me with reading this book and offering feedback. They are Becky Hensley, T.O. Weller and Julia Robinson. Your generosity of time and talent is highly valued and appreciated. I also appreciate Susan Thompson and Joanne Mintz for their valuable final proofing.

In addition, I want to thank the hundreds of followers on my blog SMART Living 365.com. It is because of you that I know what information should be included in this book. Your feedback showed me what you liked and what you found helpful, and it is my sincere hope that these words reach out and touch those who can benefit most from a simple change in heart and lifestyle.

TABLE OF CONTENTS

Introduction

"A man sooner or later discovers that he is the master-gardener of his soul, the director of his life." ~James Allen

Like so many others, I was raised believing in a golden period of life called retirement. That moment would eventually arrive after 40+ years of working and saving what money each of us could. Once there, we'd never have to work another day in our lives. And if we were smart and lucky enough, we'd have all the money we would need to finally spend our days doing whatever we wanted. After years of sacrifice and denial we'd be able enjoy the life we've been given.

Yet now that I've come within throwing distance of this cultural dream, I see things much differently. First, a large number of us haven't been lucky or smart enough to save the money we need to ever stop working completely. Second, even if we are able to stop working, many of us don't really know what to joyfully do with all that free time. Third, after waiting so long, some find our health has deteriorated to the extant that we are unable to physically do what we always dreamed of doing. And finally and most importantly, where on earth did we get the idea that putting off living a happy, engaged and fulfilled life for a possible retirement was the best way to go?

Instead I have come to believe that there is a much better path and I call that path "rightsizing." Rightsizing, as you will read about in the following pages of this book, is first taking the time to find out what it is that really brings you joy and then figuring out how to do it *right now*—today, rather than at some distant time in the future. At the same time, rightsizing is also about eliminating everything that isn't necessary or that important in your life. Ultimately, by focusing on what is important and eliminating what isn't, the path to a rightsized life is as individual as you are.

Unfortunately, the most challenging part of living a rightsized life is that no one else can give you answers. Finding out what makes you feel happy, energized and fulfilled is something only you can discover for yourself. So while this book is a collection of the best posts I have written about the topic in the last four years on my blog SMARTLiving365.com, you are going to have to do the real work.

Also, please keep in mind that many of the examples I provide are from my life and perspective. I live in a Southern California desert community that has some very unique characteristics. For example, where I live it is very common for even lower-middle class families to have a swimming pool. Plus, just about everyone has a gardener to take care of their yards. When I talk about my life, please remember that while I do enjoy many of the automatic benefits of my age and culture, I share many common realities with the majority of people who live in the U.S. But we are all slightly different and every community has its own distinctive character, so be sure to adjust accordingly.

What does a rightsized life look like? One great example I know that points to the benefits of a rightsized life is the tale of a Mexican Fisherman and a hotshot Hedge Fund Manager. Even though I've read and told this story many times, I happen to know it helps to read it over and over again.

It begins when the stressed out Hedge Fund Manager forces himself to take a vacation to a quaint seaside village in Mexico to "relax." While taking a lunchtime walk by the harbor, he is horrified to see a Mexican man lounging next to his fishing boat smoking a cigar in the middle of the day.

"It's the middle of the day. Why aren't you out fishing?" questioned the Hedge Fund Manager.

"Because I've caught enough fish for today," replied the Mexican with a smile.

"But it's still early. Surely you could catch a lot more?" exclaimed the Manager with a mind clearly working overtime.

The Mexican shrugged and explained that he had plenty to support his families' immediate needs.

"But what do you do with your extra time?" asked the

mystified Manager.

The Fisherman smiled and said, "Oh, I sleep late, fish a little, play with my children, take siesta with my wife Maria, then stroll into the village each evening where I sip wine and play guitar with my friends. I have a full, happy and busy life."

"But if you kept fishing you could earn a lot more money," replied the Hedge Fund Manager with growing excitement. "Then you could buy a bigger boat and go into deeper waters for even more fish. Once you catch enough fish, you could possibly buy another boat and so on and so forth. Before you know it, you could own a fleet of fishing boats and then even open your own cannery. After that, you would not only control the product, but the processing and distribution. Of course, then you would need to leave this small village, move to Mexico City and then eventually LA. From there you could run your ever expanding empire."

"But then what?" asked the Mexican with a frown.

"Oh, that's the best part," answered the Hedge Fund Manager. When the time is right you would announce an IPO, sell your company stock to the public, and become an extremely wealthy man. You'd make millions."

"Millions?" asked the Fisherman. "Then what?"

Surprised, the Manager paused and thought a moment before softly saying, "Then you could retire and move to a small scenic fishing village where you could sleep late, fish a little, play with your kids, take siesta with your wife, and then stroll into the village in the evenings where you could sip wine and play your guitar with your friends."

I don't have all the answers for my own life, let alone yours. But I do believe that taking the time to consider what is most important and what really matters can improve our lives no matter where we are on the path. With that in mind, I am extremely hopeful that some of the examples I'm including in this book will encourage you to take the steps necessary to start rightsizing your life. Then, should you decide to retire—or not—you will make your choices from a place of clarity and awareness. Regardless of whether the retirement dream from our youth exists as a possibility for us, I honestly believe we have more options than we know and we have more freedom than we often realize. Best of all, we don't have to wait. We can rightsize right NOW.

Chapter One

A Journey of Rightsizing, or How Big Is Big Enough?

"At each point in our lives, we are at a crossroads. We are the fruit of our past and we are the architects of our future... If you want to know your past, look at your present circumstances. If you want to know your future, look at what is in your mind." ~ Mathieu Ricard

In 2010, my husband Thom and I bought a new home in the "village area" of La Quinta, CA. We called it an experiment because we weren't sure if we could live in a house that was nearly a 1,000 square feet smaller than the one we had before. Never mind that the new house had 1,375 square feet with three bedrooms, two bathrooms and was plenty large enough based on comparables around the world. But with huge changes happening in the economy, and our personal growing awareness in the environmental movement, Thom and I felt it was time to discover if the American obsession with size was just a habit we'd adopted or a true necessity. What we've come to know during the last five years is that smaller is plenty big enough, especially when it fits perfectly within your needs.

One of the first unexpected responses we got from our experiment was reaction from others. When people heard we were selling our previous home and moving to a different area of La Quinta, we were asked several times if "everything was all right?" Some people seemed to assume that because we were selling in a down real estate market that something must be wrong—and some seemed to assume that because we were buying a smaller, visually less impressive house, that something must be really wrong. Without being said, the implication was that the size and stature of our home was being used as an indicator of our well-being or success.

When did that happen? When did everyone start using the size and quality of a person's home to evaluate the family's happiness and prosperity? I think we all know on some level that such a superficial comparison has nothing to do with true happiness or contentment. After all, if you ask most people what is most important to them, no one will admit it is the size of their house or car or television set. Still, much of the time, if anyone makes a move that seems contrary to "bigness" or even pauses on the ladder of success, observers tend to think something is abnormal or wrong. Maybe it is time to rethink that reaction.

So, what were the personal intentions behind our experiment? One goal was the quest for fewer hassles. As any one who has one knows, the bigger the home, the more time it takes to take care of it. Sure we had lots of nice furniture and a big lovely yard with a pool and spa. But based on how much the two of us actually used some of those amenities, they just didn't seem that important to us as time went by. We also decided that although our mortgage on the bigger house was something we were able to easily maintain, the thought of

8

owning a home completely free and clear seemed daringly extravagant. Lastly, we wanted a home in a certain neighborhood that offered dozens of free benefits and the only ones available in our price range were more modest in size. Again, the trade-off seemed beneficial.

Five years later, we fit perfectly in our home with no regrets. Not only does our home contain everything we need, we also love our neighbors. One thing we never expected was the advantage of living in a denser neighborhood and being physically closer to people. We feel much more a part of a community and enjoy spending time walking and participating in everything that happens around us in a much more personal way. Daily, we can walk or bike to grocery stores, the library, restaurants, parks, and all sorts of other outlets. Instead of merely living in the suburbs, we now live amongst friends.

Interestingly enough, once we cleaned out the excess from our previous home, we found our new home was plenty big enough for all the stuff we really wanted and needed in our lives. Again, the more stuff you have the more it has to be cleaned, taken care of and maintained. Now, instead of having to manage and take care of a bigger home and yard, we get to spend that excess time doing things we enjoy.

Lastly, by buying a home that we could purchase free and clear we have created a freedom in our lives that was unexpected. While we realize that not everyone is in the same financial position, it is drilled into most of us (especially those of us who come from the real estate field) that buying as big a home as possible with a mortgage and then using it as a write-off is as American as apple pie. Trust me, the freedom that comes from not having to make a house or rent payment month after month after month is incomparable. Not only do we not have a house payment, we are entirely debt free and our smaller home uses much less utilities and therefore, carries much less cost. All the money we used to pay out for mortgage, higher taxes, higher insurance, maintenance and stuff from our previous home allows us to travel and do things that feed our passions—not pay bills.

While I am obviously overjoyed to have right-sized our home and life as we have (can you see me smiling?), I don't share it to brag. Instead, wouldn't it be nice if we all started talking about and discussing the freedom, advantages and joy that come from living within our means? What if we ignored obvious displays of grandeur and bigness and instead looked with admiration on people living lives of passion and purpose—in a sustainable and moderate way? What would happen if we started congratulating each other for being able to relax and enjoy what we had, rather than working our butts off to pay for stuff we don't really need? What if we all started making choices and decisions that were based on living SMART instead of living big?

Much of the time, sustainability means taking care of the planet—cleaning up after yourself and not using more than you need—being eco-friendly in all that you say and do. However, what I have come to learn is that sustainability starts at home, literally and figuratively. I now believe that sustainability is living within your means, and loving what you have instead of always striving for something bigger and better. When it comes down to it, having the space to "mentally" breathe is much SMARTer than having extra rooms in your house.

Chapter Two

Rightsizing vs. Downsizing By The Numbers

"Have the courage to follow your heart and intuition. They somehow already know what you truly want to become. Everything else is secondary." ~Steve Jobs

Last month, Thom came across an article in the **Wall Street Journal (WSJ)** with a headline that said, *"**Everybody Says You Should Downsize. Everybody May Be Wrong.**"* We both found that statement to be so incredulous that we had to reread it. And we weren't alone in our surprise. Most of the other comments online also questioned many of the negative points offered in the article. Clearly the author herself had not downsized, and it was also obvious that her focus came from an outdated definition of the concept. Naturally, that got me thinking that maybe most of us approach the topic from the wrong direction to begin with. Instead of thinking of it as "down" sizing—maybe we should consider it to be "right"sizing. And once we get the label right—it is much easier to consider the real benefits that come from living a lifestyle that is rightsized from the beginning.

Thom and I didn't start out searching for a way to rightsize. In fact, it wasn't until about five years ago that the shift inside us began. Just like many people at the time, we never actually considered that there was a difference. Up until that point, we were like many Americans who thought success was having a large impressive house, all the money necessary to buy things we enjoyed, and work that would continue to make more and more money to keep that lifestyle growing. But what might have made us different from many of our fellow Americans was the awareness that at some point something had to give. Growth without adjustment is unsustainable. Striving for more and more at all cost is unnatural. Breathing in, without breathing out, just doesn't work for very long.

In 2007, we suspected that the American economy was headed for trouble. Most people we knew were deeply in debt. Real estate prices had exploded to unrealistic highs with mortgage terms that few people could ever pay back. The average square footage on most homes had swelled from 1,400 in 1970, to 2,700 in 2009. By the same token, both men and women in America weigh, on the average, about 20 pounds more than they did back in 1990. Our country was addicted to bigger, more, and growth at all cost.

Maybe because Thom and I have been self-employed for most of our lives and have spent quite a bit of time on self-awareness and reflection, we were better able to see what was heading our way and embrace the shift looming on the horizon. Whenever anyone senses something like that happening, it's best to figure out a way to flow with, or ride, the wave that is surely coming.

That's when Thom and I sat down and started redefining what was important to us and where it was we wanted to go. Thom has always been attracted to the green and sustainable movement, and particularly how that fits within the real estate world. He convinced me that energy conservation and sustainability needed to be part of the future of our country, the planet, and our lives.

We also realized that having a big house in the suburbs packed with amenities wasn't really that important to us. Instead we craved community, walkability and connection. The more specific we got about what was important to us and what we wanted to experience in our lives on a regular basis, the simpler the solution. Rightsizing was the path to creating a lifestyle that uniquely fit what our hearts desired.

While that explanation might make it sound like it was an easy solution—it really wasn't. It took several years and is still being fine-tuned nearly every day. Truthfully, in the beginning we thought we'd just scale our lifestyle back a bit. While our mortgage was never excessive, our original goal was to cut it in half. But as time went by, and we got more and more clear about what it was we *really* wanted, the idea of having a home with no mortgage or association dues became more and more desirable. That decision saved us $1,600 per month.

To be honest, in the beginning some of it felt like compromise. I was under the impression that going from a big house to less than 1,400 sq. ft. would be unworkable. But when we found a house in a neighborhood that we really liked—that contained a number of benefits that we were convinced were highly valuable to us—we bought a house at nearly half the size of our previous one and have been happy ever since. Something I discovered was that even more important than square footage of a house is the layout and location. If you take the time to find a layout that works for you, the size is usually secondary. And if the neighborhood/location is good and close to things you find important, then the value is greatly enhanced.

Another thing that most of us ignore is that the larger your home, the more you need to furnish and maintain. A more compact house doesn't need to be filled with as much stuff (there is NOWHERE to put it!) When you take the time to carefully furnish and decorate your house with only a few things that you love and need, it frees up both your mind and your heart to focus on those things that bring you happiness.

In addition to needing less inside your new smaller home is the advantage of far less maintenance and utility costs. Most people seldom consider the true costs of what it will take to cool, heat or light up their property until after those first few bills start arriving. Not only did our smaller home come with smaller utility costs, we have also been able to add a number of energy saving features (like solar) that have practically eliminated our energy costs. By rightsizing our house size, we've managed to save another $250 a month in that department. And don't forget taxes, insurance and general maintenance. Those amounts save us another $250 every single month.

Something else that felt a bit like a compromise in the beginning was the small yard that came with our new house. The yard at the last house was twice the size and contained a lovely pool, spa and grassy lawn. (Remember in the beginning I mentioned that I live in a desert climate so pools are the norm and nearly everyone has a gardener to maintain their heavily-watered lawn.) While it was certainly beautiful and I was quite proud to own the previous property—a person shouldn't forget the ongoing expenses to maintain those amenities. Specifically, that previous yard w/pool cost us on average around $550 per month. Truth be told, we seldom swam in the pool or used the yard. On top of that, we routinely spent time and energy managing the gardeners, pool man and ongoing repairs.

At our new house we designed our desert-scape yard that we maintain ourselves. After taking the time to create it right from the beginning, it is not only beautiful, but we feel more connected to it than our previous yard because we take care of it ourselves. Sure it's nice to be able to have a gardener, a pool man and other helpers, but all that takes both money AND time.

So how much did we save? Here is a breakdown of the amount we save every month by living a "rightsized" lifestyle. (FYI…I'm not trying to boast by sharing these numbers but rather encourage people to be honest about what their lifestyle is actually costing them. With the right knowledge it is easier to make changes.)

Actual money saved:

- Previous mortgage: $1,600
- Pool, spa & yard   550
- Utilities & maintenance   250
- Taxes & insurance   250
- Total savings $2,650 or $31,800 /year!

Of course the biggest point I want to make about rightsizing is not just about the money. Sure it's nice to have an extra $31,800 every single year to spend on investments or other things we truly enjoy, but the best benefit is how liberating the experience of living debt free turns out to be. By not having the additional financial commitment of over $30,000 per year hanging over our head for things we didn't really need and had grown tired of caring for, we freed ourselves to use that same amount of money to follow our dreams and desires and/or to be of help to causes we believe in supporting.

Other highlights from the change include now living in a neighborhood that is tremendously rewarding. Our current neighborhood offers a handful of free amenities that we consider much more desirable than our previous yard and bigger home. We also have a great deal more free time to devote to exercise, creativity and relationships that we would have unknowingly forfeited to just maintaining a larger lifestyle.

So why do people call such a positive change "downsizing?" As that article in the WSJ pointed out, calling the change a downsize puts the focus on sacrificing and giving up. Rather than focus on the positive, the idea of downsizing is that something must be "wrong" and you are only doing it because you have to do it.

Instead we prefer the idea of rightsizing as a conscious choice for a better lifestyle that more closely fits you and your family in the best way possible. It has nothing to do with constant striving toward more or bigger, or putting yourself at risk with unsustainable debt. It has nothing to do with stressing yourself to the max by trying to outdo your neighbors, family or co-workers. Instead, rightsizing is about being honest with yourself enough to figure out what you are spending money on and whether that money is worth the time, effort and spirit you invest earning it. Best of all, rightsizing is about finding what brings your life meaning, makes you smile, and allows you to sleep well and deeply every single night. If you don't have that now, maybe it's time to rightsize your life.

Chapter Three

Rightsizing Your Way To Retirement—Getting Started

"If you are going to retire from anything,
retire from fear and illusion." ~ Alan Cohen

Retirement is a big topic for many of us in midlife. The usual approach is to figure out how much money you can possibly save up so that you can continue the lifestyle you have created for you and your family. The other approach is to downsize and sacrifice so you can live on whatever you think you'll be forced to get by living on and with. There IS another way. Several years ago Thom and I came up with what is a middle (and we think *better*) way that is seldom mentioned. That way is to "rightsize" your life as soon as possible. Then whether you choose to finally retire, or decide you will continue creating in some capacity for as long as you live— your life will be filled with qualities and activities that bring you happiness, purpose, and peace of mind.

So what is rightsizing and why will that help? To keep things simple I came up with two main steps to creating a rightsized life. The first step is to approach rightsizing from a psychological and holistic perspective for creating a quality life. Here are what I believe to be the critical questions to ask yourself:

* What kind of a life do you want to live? Okay, I'll admit that this one sounds obvious. But I'm constantly amazed that more people I know don't seem to have a clue. Life seems to happen "to" them and they spend all of their time and energy reacting to whatever comes along.

Of course Thom and I started out that way ourselves. We *sort of* had an idea what we wanted, but we were as susceptible as most people to cultural messages telling us that the way to be happy was to make lots of money and buy lots of stuff. Still, something within Thom knew he wanted to be self-employed at just about any cost. Fortunately, finding work was never a problem for either of us. However, finding work that would pay us enough to live on was something we struggled with for many years.

Gradually we developed the talents and consciousness that enabled us to create work that paid well. And because we had lived modestly for so long, we didn't go too crazy buying a bunch of stuff on credit or a humongous house that sucked up every bit of that income. However, although we managed to live within our means, we still spent pretty much every dollar we made, and our lifestyle came at a cost of a mortgage, plenty of bills and corresponding stress.

Then five years ago we came to the conclusion that the debt we were carrying around was sucking all the enjoyment out of our lives. Sure we had a nice house, nice cars, nice stuff—but at what price? Was all that stuff really that important to us?

So for the next six months we sat down together, did a lot of soul searching, and started imagining a life filled with activities and experiences we felt would bring us happiness, purpose and peace of mind. We've since learned that taking the time and being clear about this is essential. What kind of life do *you* want to live? Without looking at how others do it, or watching a TV program and dreaming about it, sit down with a piece of paper and *really* figure out what's important to you.

* If you did retire, or could do whatever you wanted all day, what would you do? A friend named Pete loves restoring old motorcycles. When he retired he bought a home where he built a large motorcycle shop attached to his home and he works day and night on those motorcycles. He also purchased a home near a popular and spectacular location for riding motorcycles, so when not working on them he spends time riding them. By deciding what was important and what he loved spending time on, he has rightsized his life.

You've probably heard the question: What would you do if you didn't have to make money doing it? This is the same question with a slightly different perspective. It asks, what would you like to spend your days doing if you didn't have to worry about money? The real answer to that question can tell you more than you realize.

We all need purpose and meaning to live a happy and fulfilled life. Unfortunately, some people seem to think that merely leaving an unhappy workplace will make them happy. Wrong! Lazing around, playing golf or bouncing grandkids on your lap might work for a while, but unless those activities are bound up in your sense of fulfilment, purpose and happiness, boredom will likely set in—and yes, kids do grow up and don't like to be bounced!

* Make a list of all the things you love doing that don't cost a dime. When you think about it, we aren't asked this question very often. Most of the time, we are being sold on new exciting items that we supposedly need to buy before we can even think about being happy. But chances are good that there are numerous things that you enjoy doing that cost nothing. For example, a few free things that I love to do are: 1) take a walk or hike with Thom and Kloe (our dog); 2) go to free community concerts or lectures; 3) sit and write an interesting blog post; 4) work in my garden; 5) catch up with friends; etc. Okay your turn. What do you like doing that doesn't cost you a thing?

* Figure out what activities stimulate you so that you could do them for hours on end. For example, I LOVE to plan vacations. I can sit for hours on the Internet figuring out a weekend trip out of town or a month-long vacation. In fact, I get about as much pleasure from planning vacations as I do actually taking them. Another friend of mine loves to cook and will spend hours pouring over recipes planning healthy and inexpensive meals for her friends and family. What is it that grabs your attention and keeps it occupied for hours?

* What experiences are you most excited to tell others about? Photography has always been something Thom enjoys. After investing in a camera (and no it doesn't have to be the most impressive one out there) he spends hours taking photos, working with photos, reading about photos online and studying how other people do it—and then he loves to talk to other people about photography. What is it that YOU love to tell others about?

* Do you like where you live? Where else have you always dreamed of living? One thing I've noticed about people is that we all enjoy different locations. Some people prefer cold weather. Me? I could live the rest of my life without it. Some like the desert, some like the ocean, some like the mountains. Figuring out the place you feel best is simple— having the courage to move there, no matter what, is the challenge. Oh, and don't pick a location just because you want to be near someone else like family or a new lover. What happens if they move away or lose interest? Where is your *place* on the planet?

Another side to this question is how does your living location fit your dream lifestyle. For example, even though Thom and I used to live in a very nice "gated community," it actually felt very divisive. When we bought our new home, we wanted to live close to a local "village" area where we could walk and bike to stores, the library, restaurants, parks and all sorts of other services. What's important to you? Do you need to be out in the country so you can have a huge garden? Is seclusion important to you? Again, never settle on a location because it SOUNDS good or worse yet—because you can buy it cheap. Instead, seek out what will make you smile on a regular basis.

* How do you like to give back to others? As has been said, those who are most happy in life have figured out a way to be of service to other people. What service have you provided to others in the past that not only makes you feel good about yourself, but is fun, inspiring and uplifting in the process? Getting in touch with this quality adds immense value to your life and doesn't usually cost a cent.

* What kind of people inspire, uplift and make you feel healthy, happy and valuable? There are dozens of reasons to select a location and live around people who feed your soul. Science now shows if you hang out with overweight people you are very likely to be heavy yourself. By the same token, if you hang around unhappy, unmotivated, unloved people, you too will feel that way much of the time. Don't assume only a significant other or family will love you into your future—make the kind of friends that bring out the very best in you, make you smile and lift you up

As I write out these questions I'm aware of how basic they seem. I'm also aware that so many people I know really don't take the time to answer them. But remember—THE ANSWERS DETERMINE OUR LIVES!!! This is what will either become a happy memory—or a life of regret. Taking the time to focus in on what it is that will give our lives purpose and positive direction is critical.

Unfortunately, we aren't taught this and I can't remember my parents even suggesting that it would be good to know. Many in the generations before us did this automatically, but most of it didn't pass on to the present times. But regardless of what you did or didn't do in the past, right here—right now, things can change. With the right motivation every one of us can create a life that is happier, more purposeful and stress free. In other words, we can create a rightsized life starting this minute before or during retirement.

Chapter Four

Rightsizing Your Way To Retirement—The Next Step

"It isn't what you have, or who you are, or where you are, or what you are doing that makes you happy or unhappy. It is what you think about."
~Dale Carnegie

Back in our twenties, my husband Thom and I wanted to be millionaires. TV shows like **Lifestyles of the Rich & Famous and Who Wants To Be A Millionaire?** fuelled the desire to amass our fortune. Then somewhere along the way someone really wise asked Thom, "Why a millionaire?" and forced him to consider what he meant by that idea. For the first time, Thom began listing experiences and feelings that he hoped to achieve if and when he/we became millionaires. To which his friend said something like, "So it's really the feelings and experiences you want—not the money itself?"

From that moment forward, we began realizing that the labels of being rich, poor or somewhere in-between had little to do with the actual quality or experience of our lives. In fact, the things we thought most important could be realized with far less income than we ever imagined. That's why through the years we've come to believe that "rightsizing" is a much better way to describe the unique and priceless lifestyle that brings you happiness, purpose and peace of mind regardless of your age. Once you have that clear picture of what brings you a happy and quality lifestyle, you can begin to figure out the next step of where and how money fits into your life.

As I mentioned in the last chapter where I covered some of the psychological aspects of rightsizing, the first step is always figuring out what it is that will bring you closer to living a happy, purposeful and low-stress life. Once you've got that figured out, the next step is determining the trade offs and costs that such a lifestyle requires. Chances are, if you work with financial or retirement planners they will tell you an amount of money you'll need to come up with to continue living the lifestyle you are currently living. Their work is a cookie-cutter approach that implies that people are humanoids who all want the same things, never change, and are addicted to "more."

But the best questions are much deeper than just maintaining the status quo. Rightsizing suggests that the best lifestyle is one that is juicy, deeply satisfying, emotionally rewarding with minimal stress, filled with purpose and creativity, and as unique and special as each individual. Once each of us arrives at a clearer picture of who we are and what really makes *us* happy, then we can start seeking ways to experience that on a regular basis.

Here's a good place to start:

#1 Sit down and list *exactly* (line by line) what you are spending to maintain your current home—specifically mortgage, insurance, utilities, taxes, yard, maintenance, etc. If you are renting, list every expense like rental rate and utilities. I know, it's not a fun job but it is very important to be honest and aware of what it is you are spending your money on— everything from silly stuff to big and important things.

For example, before Thom and I made our big move from a large suburban home to a home almost half the size, we discovered that we were spending almost $40,000 extra every year to live in that house with those amenities. Because we had also taken the time beforehand to write out what was very important to us to live a quality life—we realized that a big house wasn't on the list and didn't mean that much to us. Instead we discovered that we could better use that nearly $40,000 in ways that would double and triple our happiness quotient. Also keep in mind that if you can rent a place that suits you at a fraction of the price to own, that might be a great alternative.

#2 Look at your vehicles and add up all the costs associated with them. I mean all costs—car payment, gas, taxes, insurance, maintenance, and upkeep. Now look at your list of things you feel is important to a quality life and see where those cars fit into it. Do you really need that many cars or those models? I know several people who are slaves to large, expensive, name-brand cars just because they think it adds to their prestige or image. Face it—the only people who care how many you have or what kind of car you drive are people who are also worried about what everyone thinks. The quality of your life and experiences ultimately has very little to do with what anyone thinks of you, and lots to do with any trade-offs you're willing to make to drive (and own) certain types of vehicles.

#3 What kind of debt are you carrying around? You've already done some of this with your home and car, but what are your other debts. Credit cards? Lines of credit? Purchases on time? List each one with both the balance and the average payment you make each month. Then list them in order of the "stress level" each of them brings. If you struggle every month to pay your credit cards those would go to the top of your list. Again, knowing which causes the most stress is illuminating.

#4 Now make a list of every single on-going expense you have every month. Start with all your home costs that you've already calculated, plus your car expenses and then keep going. List how much you routinely spend on everything: food, entertainment, phone, cable, utilities, insurance, education, coffee, children, etc. List everything. Take a day or two to do this because if you dwell on it you will come up with more and more things you conveniently forget about but still spend.

Once you have that list, look through it and rate every single cost on a 1 to 10 basis for how much it adds to your life in terms of quality. For example—take cable TV. I happen to watch more TV than I need to, but I also enjoy some of the programming that I watch. However, if I were to "rate" it honestly, the cost of my cable TV on a 1 to 10 scale would likely be around a 6. I could do without it; especially if there was something I was denying myself that I would enjoy more. Knowing its importance to me tells me a lot about my life.

All of the above questions attempt to clarify what you are currently spending money on and how important –or not important—those things are to your idea of a quality life. Now that you have pinpointed where your money is going—now is the time to ask yourself the following:

A) When I look back on all the questions I answered in the last chapter—how much of my money am I spending doing those things? If you say you love fixing motorcycles and riding them as much as possible, but never seem to have time to do it, that's a good place to start. If you love to cook but are always too tired after slaving at a job you dislike, then you need to look at that too. Are you spending your time, energy and money doing things like shopping when you would just as soon be going to a free community concert or lecture?

B) How do you feel about your current job? Do you stay in your job only because you are "waiting" to retire? Can you see from some of the other experiences that your current job might actually be costing you more of both money and life energy than it's worth?

C) Do you continually reward yourself for working at a job you don't like? You know what I mean right? You buy yourself a Venti Frappuccino on the way home from work because you had a long hard day. Not only are you spending five bucks, but you're ingesting a large amount of sugar and caffeine. Or maybe you shop. Do you buy that extra pair of shoes because they're cute, and it makes you feel better about the fact that your boss yelled at you that day? Do you often spend money you don't have just to take away the pain or boredom you are feeling? Eventually, the cost of those expenses will cause even more stress that needs to be addressed.

D) List what you could eliminate today that would make you feel freer and less stressed out—then put them in order. If you are going to a job that feels like a noose around your neck, that might be number one. Or are you struggling every month to make credit card bills—or a mortgage payment? List the things that would make your life feel great if they were gone.

Once you've come up with that list—compare it to the list of things you came up with in the last chapter of rightsizing your life. Say you've become aware that your current debt level is sucking the very life out of you. Obviously, a first step would be to put most of your efforts into paying that particular debt off. Sure it might require extra time and energy—but remember, if you have a good idea of things you can do that are free that make you even more happy—you can start adding those to your life whenever possible.

I recommend that you go for the big stuff first. Like I mentioned before, Thom and I realized that our house took a huge chunk of money that we would rather spend doing other things. We also had three cars at the time. Letting go of one of those vehicles allowed us to free up money, time and energy.

E) What would it take for you to be debt-free? I know that lots of people can't imagine being debt free so this might seem like a bit of a stretch. But if you take the time there might be some way you could see yourself free of debt and living a much happier life. Sure, you might have to save and be thriftier for a number of years to pay off your mortgage—or you might simply be able to sell what you have and scale down to what you really need to accomplish the same goal. For Thom and me, one of the most rewarding aspects of rightsizing has been achieved by going completely debt free. Honestly, it was not an easy thing to do, but even if it takes a number of years like it did with us—it *can* be done if you really want to achieve this goal. Do you?

There are actually dozens of more questions you could ask yourself that would help simplify your finances and rightsize your lifestyle, but the above are a great place to start. If you get bogged down or have a difficult time staying optimistic through the process, I recommend that you go back to the last chapter and remember all of the things that are truly important to you. Whenever we spend time focusing on the activities and qualities that make our lives meaningful and worth living, we are uplifted and rejuvenated. That is the power of rightsizing—and it is always within our reach.

So what does all this have to do with retirement? In case you haven't guessed yet, when we rightsize our lives we are well on our way to the ultimate freedom of being able to live as we choose—before or during retirement.

Chapter Five

Step Three To Rightsize Your Life Right Now!

I don't want to get to the end of my life and find that I lived just the length of it. I want to have lived the width of it as well. ~ Diane Ackerman

If you've read the previous two chapters I hope you've picked up that rightsizing is actually a way of life—at any age—not just for those entering retirement. Again, I define rightsizing as creating a life that uniquely fits and satisfies you and your family with the greatest amount of joy and contentment and the least amount of stress or worry. While the lifestyle offers tremendous benefits to those of us in midlife or contemplating retirement, every person who is interested in a more simple, meaningful, and happy life will benefit.

Step one in this series focused on the consciousness behind a rightsized life, while step two got down to the nitty-gritty of finances. In this, the final step to rightsizing your life, I want to throw out a few random thoughts that can help to increase your understanding and awareness.

1) Find role models for the kind of life you want to live. If you watch a lot of TV, chances are the role models you find there are living extravagant, overly dramatic and unrealistic lifestyles. What we can't see is the day-to-day pressures many of those "personalities" go through, struggling to pay their bills or learning to live with other people in a loving and meaningful way. On close examination, the "lifestyles of the rich and famous" come with their own set of complications and headaches.

I suggest instead that you look around at the people you know (or maybe have only recognized from a distance) who are living a happy, content and stress-less lifestyle—and then follow their lead. It's also likely that if you ask those people how they have accomplished their lifestyle, they will be more than happy to share with you what has worked for them. Gradually, as you surround yourself with others who are living the lifestyle you long for, not only will it become easier, your contentment will grow.

2) Research locations to find the rightsized place to live.

There are a number of people in retirement who are convinced that they can only afford to retire in another country to happily live the lifestyle they crave. While I have nothing against living anywhere you've always wanted to live—I know you don't have to go international to live a simple, rewarding and relatively inexpensive lifestyle.

By my own example, I live in Southern California in a resort type location and we've worked to drastically reduce our living expenses. Truthfully we planned it that way. Based upon some of our previous choices and tradeoffs, we could not live anywhere in the world for less money while enjoying our high quality lifestyle, than where we live right now. Sure we had to scale down the size and scope of our home as well as forgo certain amenities—but by carefully "rightsizing" we made sure that our home offered dozens of alternate low or no cost benefits that made the trade-off easy in our minds. Every single one of us has that option, but it does require intention.

3) When you love your work (or life) you'll automatically reduce the need to spend money. I think if you pay attention, you will find that people who dislike what they do tend to spend more money trying to find happiness to offset the struggle/stress they have at work (life). On the flip side, when you love your work (life) you will spend more time doing that—and you'll be much less likely to spend money self-medicating by shopping and buying needless stuff to overcome your unhappiness.

No matter what your age, start looking for work (or life practices) that satisfy your soul on at least a few levels. The more your efforts provide you with satisfaction and bring meaning and purpose to your existence, the more you will be able to recognize the simple and everyday things that offer you the greatest happiness and peace.

4) The only person who fixes your income is you. Far too many people complain about their income—especially many who are retired and call it "fixed." But the question remains, *who* fixed your income? Unless you were forced to quit or retire due to health reasons, there are still dozens of ways to continue to contribute to the world in meaningful ways. Besides, if you make an effort to find work that you enjoy and feel it has meaning and purpose—you might be surprised at the unique opportunities that show up and how much extra income can flow into your life.

5) Make gratitude a habit that you practice every day. While I realize that this suggestion could be added to just about every article I post on my blog—it HAS to be included when writing about rightsizing. Not only does gratitude make you feel better about yourself and your circumstances the minute you start doing it, it also puts the focus on all the incredible good filling your life right now. The big problem is that we often tend to overlook and become conditioned to everything that is good and working well in our lives—and let the problems occupy our main attention. Instead, when you make gratitude your habit, your mind zeros in on the good and overlooks the less desirable. That, my friends, leads to a much happier rightsized life.

6) Storyboard the rightsized life you want to experience.
Ever heard of storyboards? A storyboard (sometimes called a vision board) is a visual way to subliminally remind ourselves of what we would like to experience in our life. How do you do it? Get a big piece of construction paper, fill it with photos and words that describe your rightsized life in five years from now, and then hang it on a wall in your house where you will walk past it every single day. We hang ours right next to the garage door entrance to our house.

Thom and I have made several storyboards throughout our lives. The latest one was made right before we decided to rightsize our home and start practicing a more simple and sustainable lifestyle five years ago. Of course that didn't mean we wanted to sacrifice—my storyboard was loaded with fun events and travel opportunities. But to fulfil our rightsized ideas we added things like solar for our home, a hybrid car, a raised bed garden, and certain technology tools that make our lives more enjoyable. It also included pictures of us involved in healthy activities, having friends over for dinner, going dancing and taking walks in nature. Five years later, just about everything on that board is now a part of our lives. Currently we are working on a new board to help us visualize the next five years. Maybe it's time for you to make one of your own.

7) Find Your Tribe. Nearly every study done on successful aging points out that those with strong social ties live longer and happier lives. My father was a great example. For most of his life he was deeply involved with the local Elks Club. While such membership organizations aren't as popular these days, it was very important for my father. I am convinced that his heavy social connection to this club contributed to his long, happy and relatively healthy life. Whether your tribe is family or friend-related it doesn't matter—what matters is that you feel connected and close to a circle of friends. Find your tribe to live a rightsized life.

8) Love the one you're with. Let's be honest here—if you aren't deeply in love with your significant other, and prefer being with that person more than anyone else, then retirement could be challenging for you. I have a difficult time understanding women who constantly complain that when their husband retired it drove them crazy. What? If you consider your partner nothing more than a bothersome roommate, that's another discussion altogether. If you really, really want to enjoy a rightsized life, make sure the one you live with is someone you prefer to be with above all others. (And yes, that means your kids or your own parents too.) Sure its great having a wonderful relationship with your children, your family and girl-friends/guy-friends, but in this day and age a live-in relationship should be a partnership of choice—not an obligation or convenience.

In the following chapters you'll see that I have more to say about rightsizing, but why not start "being the change you want to see in the world" right now? Ultimately it won't matter how many ideas I offer, if you aren't ready or don't see the value, none of this will make much difference. However, if you suspect that a life of routine and always wanting more continues to make you unhappy, or you're stressed out all the time, give these ideas some thought. And if you are considering retirement in the coming years, please remember your happiness in retirement will have less to do with how much money you have saved, than your deep awareness of what it is you value and the steps you take to enjoy it.

Eventually, I'm convinced that you'll find out, just like Thom and I did, that a SMART* and rightsized life is just the practice you need to stay happily alive for the remainder of your life.

* Because these articles originally appeared on my blog, SMART Living 365.com I routinely relate them to the SMART topics of: sustainable, meaningful, aware, responsible, and thankful.

Chapter Six

Curing Your Addiction To "More"

"Things which matter most must never be at the mercy of things which matter least." ~ Goethe

"Hi, my name is Kathy and I have been addicted to *more*." What about you? The good news is that I don't believe that any of us are powerless against it—but we do need to admit that it is a problem to begin with and be on continuous alert to its presence. But what exactly do I mean by being addicted to more, and why is it so important to recognize? Plus, why is our desire for more such an important awareness for living a rightsized life?

Just like most addictions, the addiction to more is the continued, and often compulsive, use of a behaviour or substance despite adverse consequences. So just like many substances or behaviours, "more" in some forms isn't necessarily bad, it's the continued and compulsive pursuit without balance that often leads to severe unhappiness, financial ruin and all sorts of unintended outcomes. I'm guessing that if you aren't aware of how "more" is impacting your life, there is a good chance that you too are suffering from the addiction.

But what do I mean by *more*? My definition is the continuous search for something to complete us and make us feel worthy, lovable and sufficient. That something can be all sorts of material things that are easily seen and/or measured like a bigger house, a prestigious car, another pair of expensive shoes, a bigger bank account or a higher paying job. Or "more" can be related to intangibles like educational degrees, spiritual understanding or position, being in perfect physical shape, reaching the perfect weight, the love of a child, or even needing other people's recognition. *Any time* we think we need to be something more, or have something more, or do something more in order to "complete" ourselves and be okay, we are stuck in the compulsive addiction so prevalent in our world today. Again, it's not the thing or the concept that is problematic, it is our unconscious impulses that are so destructive to a peaceful and satisfied life.

Making the problem even more complicated is that in most cases our very culture and worldview encourages the universal pursuit of more—at just about any cost. With an economy built around the idea that more is *always* better, regardless of the outcome, it's no surprise that this behaviour extends all the way down to personal finance and individual lives. We believe that businesses and corporations must always be growing their income and their productivity. Likewise, we grow up believing that it's somehow un-American to be content and happy with who you are and what you have. We drive ourselves, our friends, our children and our lives with the idea that it is lazy, or unworthy or _____ (you fill in the blank) if we stop for a moment to enjoy where we are, accept ourselves as we are, and take a break.

Want to know if you have this addiction? Here's a short quiz that may help:

1) Your child tells you he/she doesn't want to go to college because what he/she really wants to be a rapper. Do you:

a) Ask them if they are nuts and question how do they expect to eat?

b) Grit your teeth, let them do what they want, and NEVER tell any friends or family what your child is really doing?

c) Insist they go to college first so they have a way to make money to fall back on when the rapper thing doesn't work out?

d) Encourage them to live their dream as long as it fulfils them and they can responsibly take care of themselves?

2) You are walking by a store and see that perfect something (whatever it is that you collect or absolutely love) on sale at 50% off. You know it is a fantastic price but you also know you don't need it and really can't afford it at the moment. Do you:

a) Buy it anyway because you're saving so much money?

b) Not buy it but feel cranky and depressed for days without it?

c) Try to guilt someone who loves you into buying it for you so you don't have to buy it yourself?

d) Accept that you don't need it and save your money for another time.

3) You are finally in the position to buy a house. You look at several you like but one stands out because it is slightly more impressive looking and bigger than what you really need. Do you:

a) Justify to yourself that a bigger and more prestigious house is a better investment?

b) Rationalize why you deserve such a house regardless of the cost?

c) Not buy it but regret it for the rest of your life?

d) Not buy it because a bigger house will stress your finances more than you'd like, admit you really don't need that extra space in the first place, and recognize you don't need to impress others ever?

4) You're offered a new job that pays you a lot more money, but you have to move to a city/place you don't really like and work for a company that you believe is untrustworthy. Do you:

a) Take the job because your goal in life has always been to make that much money?

b) Take the job and then go out and buy yourself that expensive new car that you've always wanted to offset what you have to give up?

c) Don't take the job but let your family and current employer know how much you've sacrificed just for them?

d) Not take the job knowing that you'd never sell your soul to a company you didn't trust or move to a place you didn't like just for more money.

5) You start a blog writing about things you really care about. Even though your blog takes a while to draw a small following, you receive a number of benefits from your project that are immensely gratifying. Then a blogging expert recommends you start blogging in a different way that is contrary to how you've done it, but guarantees that you will "grow more numbers." Do you:

a) Make all changes the expert recommends because the whole point of your blog is to have more followers?

b) Ignore the expert, continue to blog your own way, but hire an advertising company to promote your blog to get more followers?

c) Give up blogging altogether and go start a new project that pays better and has a better following?

d) Consider the changes and recommendations, but stay true to yourself and your intentions for your blog, regardless of what the expert suggests or whether you get more followers.

Obviously, the last answer to every one of the above questions is the one that stays true to you, regardless of the lure of "more." And even though none of the above may apply to you directly, I'm hopeful that they at least illustrate how often, and in how many ways, people routinely believe that "more" is better. I am personally attempting to recognize how many ways I, and others, routinely suggest that "more" is superior to any other action. It is especially prevalent in all advertising, but it also sneaks into our conversations with others and most especially into our expectations of those around us and ourselves.

The thing is, once we recognize why we so often choose "more" as a way to feel good we can start becoming consciously aware of what it is that we are really wanting in that moment. A lot of the time we usually just want to know and believe that we are good enough, worthy and sufficient just as we are. In the end, you don't have to be *more* of anything—except yourself.

Of course, as I said above, there may be times when striving for more is appropriate and beneficial to your life. Again, going for more is not the problem; making it unconscious and unbalanced is what creates an unhealthy addiction. When we bring our thoughts, desires and motivations out into the open and learn to appreciate all the good we have in our life right now, we are living a SMART and rightsized life.

Chapter Seven

Action Steps to Rightsize Your Health And Well-being

"Growing old is not an option. We don't have a choice. But we do have choices that will greatly affect our quality of life for the rest of our life."
~Henry K. Hebeler

A couple of years ago Thom and I started using the word "rightsizing" to help define our new lifestyle. By downscaling and simplifying our home, managing our finances, focusing on what gives purpose and meaning to our daily experience, and eliminating the unnecessary, we have gradually rightsized almost every area of our life. It was only recently that I realized that in many ways we have also rightsized our diet, our approach to exercise, and our overall health. And while I don't consider myself an expert, I do feel that as a student of SMART I've learned a few things along the way.

With that in mind, here is a list of 25 beneficial actions we believe are useful for helping anyone rightsize their diet, exercise habits and overall health:

Diet:

1. Eliminate the stress of "dieting" and instead adjust your eating to reflect the life you want.
2. Eat only when hungry—stop when full.
3. Savor and appreciate *everything* you put in your mouth—or else don't!
4. Moderation in all things is a key to a simple and balanced way of eating.
5. Avoid consuming anything that you consider filler or empty calories. If it isn't really good for you or doesn't taste awesome don't bother with it.
6. Attempt to think of eating as something you do to maintain good health, rather than something you do to reward yourself for what you *have* to do.
7. Realize that anything you appreciate and focus on will grow in your life—so if you focus on healthy eating, that is what you will experience!
8. Eat for your body. If I've learned anything during my last 60 years it is that every single one of our bodies is unique. What might work for one doesn't necessarily work for another. Find what works best for you and then do it.

Exercise:

1. Make movement a big part of every day.
2. Find ways to move that you love doing and stop forcing yourself to move in ways you dislike.
3. Pay attention and stay aware of your exercise (or lack thereof) and the habits you've formed. Create new movement habits that make you smile.
4. Buy comfortable shoes and equipment, but do it for comfort and support and let go of how you look.
5. Stop comparing your health and your body with anyone else. Strive to be the best you that you can be.

6. Learn to listen to the messages and guidance from your body. While it can be good to stretch beyond your limitations—stop when it screams "No!"
7. Adding a dog to your life that likes exercise will help in more ways than one! Not only do they keep you moving, their mere presence lowers your stress levels.
8. Strive toward balance—physically, mentally, emotionally and spiritually.

General Health:
1. Make good health a primary objective.
2. Get the right amount of good sleep as much as possible.
3. Forget trying to be younger than you are and instead celebrate and enjoy where and who you are right now.
4. Spend as much time in nature as you can.
5. Learn to meditate (quiet and focus your mind) in a way that fits you and your lifestyle. (It's amazing what just 15 minutes a day has done for me!)
6. While only going to the doctor on a regular basis won't make you a healthy person, don't ignore their help. Get checkups regularly and use their input to help keep you on track.
7. Regular intimacy and a satisfying sex life can do wonders for you physically, mentally and emotionally.
8. Surround yourself with supportive, happy and healthy people—they will mirror back to you the way to create a similar life.
9. Find a way to give back to others—volunteer, share kindness, be compassionate. A life balanced with meaning and purpose tends to make healthier choices.

Bonus Tip: Take the time to laugh and smile as much as possible. As author and speaker Abraham-Hicks says, "Life is supposed to be fun for you!" Remember that children smile and laugh approximately 400 times a day while adults usually only manage 20 times. Ask yourself, do healthy people smile and laugh more, or does an abundance of smiling and laughing make people healthy?

I understand that most of these tips are open-ended and leave a lot to your discretion. Usually diet and exercise guides provide a list of things to do or not to do and then if you don't follow them exactly right you fail. Instead, by its nature, rightsizing is something that is unique to you alone. And because our uniqueness, the responsibility for its success lies on your shoulders. So unless you are willing to think for yourself and then make choices out of your own awareness, rightsizing your diet and exercise might not be your answer.

The good news is that once you take the time to get clear about your own rightsized diet and exercise, the stress and anxiety of trying to fit into someone else's box will fall away. I tend to believe we all spend far too much time trying to live life based on other people's terms and never take the time to create, enjoy and appreciate our own path. By rightsizing your diet and exercise, you are well on your way to living SMART 365.

Chapter Eight

Avoiding Regrets = A Happier Life

*"Making a big life change is pretty scary. But you know what's even
scarier? Regret."* ~Zig Ziglar

    A musician friend named Rudi Harst wrote a song titled,
"Shoulda, Coulda, Woulda." It's both a catchy tune and a great
reminder that feelings of regret can hold us back from living a
happy and fulfilled life. But I suspect that one reason why the
song makes us laugh and wince at the same time is because we
all wish on some level that we could go back and do one or
two things differently or make at least one *other* choice along
the line. Still, what I've discovered over the last couple of days
is that regret isn't one of those negative emotions like fear,
shame or jealousy that has little or no redeeming value. Instead,
regret can serve as a signpost for pointing out choices and
changes that can help us lead a SMART, happier and rightsized
life—365.

    Interestingly enough, regret is a little tricky to define
precisely because it isn't just an emotion. While regret elicits an
emotion, it usually comes along with a judgment or appraisal of
something—in other words a choice. In countries like the U.S.

where we have a great deal of personal freedom in education, work, and relationships, those choices can lead to feelings of regret. In countries where choice and options are limited, far fewer feelings of regret are reported.

The website Happify.com offers other interesting facts about regret, claiming that 90% of people (in the U.S. at least) admit to a major regret about something in their lives. Regrets vary at different ages and with whether you are a man or a woman. For example 44% of women have romantic regrets, while only 19% of men share that feeling. It also seems that regret is most detrimental to seniors and can lead to depression and illness. A big part of that is because many elders believe it is too late to change. In contrast, younger adults usually feel they have plenty of time to avoid and alter many of their regrets.

Another fascinating tidbit about regret is that it can occur both because of something a person did, or because of something a person didn't do—in other words, either from our actions or our inactions. According to Thomas Giloviqh and Victoria Husted Medvec from Cornell University, "Actions produce greater regret in the short term; inactions generate more regret in the long run." Beyond that, Giloviqh and Medec state, "The most common regret of action was to "[rush] in too soon." They conclude, "When people look back on their lives, it is the things they have *not* done that generate the greatest regret." In fact, over the long-term, inaction is usually regretted 75% more than action.

But there is good news. ***Harvard Healthy Publications*** explains that regret can be useful no matter what our age when faced directly. The four main benefits of regret are:

1. Allows us to make sense of our past experiences;
2. Allows us to avoid more or similar mistakes made by others or ourselves;
3. Helps us fix our missteps and guides us toward greater fulfillment; and
4. Helps us improve our relationships with others.

Because we can learn from regrets, it is extremely beneficial to recognize our own blunders and those of others. The book, ***30 Life Lessons For Living*** by Karl Pillemer, Ph.D. offers five suggestions that can help us avoid such regrets. Pillemer interviewed 1,200 senior Americans, average age 78, and they offered the following advice:

- **Always be honest, trustworthy and "fair and square."** According to Pillemer his "experts" unanimously and vehemently agreed that living otherwise leads to certain and eventual regret.
- **Say yes to opportunities.** As I mention above, most regret comes from inaction rather than our actions. As the Mark Twain quote goes, "Twenty years from now you will be more disappointed by the things you didn't do than by the ones you did do. So throw off the bowlines. Sail away from the safe harbor. Catch the trade winds in your sails. Explore. Dream. Discover."
- **Travel more.** You know I love this one! What's amazing is that most of the "experts" interviewed in the book admitted that they lived rather small and local lives, yet part of them deeply regretted not experiencing new places, new people, or new ideas. As Pillemer says, "Don't put off until tomorrow what you can do today."
- **Choose a mate with extreme care.** It's likely that the most important "choice" we make in our lives is the

person we marry. Unfortunately, according to the "experts," we usually make three big mistakes when it comes to our life partners. 1) We think love and lust are the same thing; 2) we commit out of desperation; 3) we commit without thinking much at all. Any one of the three can lead to regret.

- **Say it now.** According to Pillemer, "…when it comes to deep, long-lasting regret, the experts pointed instead toward things left unsaid." Their advice? "If you have something to say to someone, do it before it's too late."

Another set of suggestions came from "experts" profiled by palliative care nurse and author Bonnie Ware in her book, *The Top Five Regrets of The Dying*. They are:

1. **I wish I'd had the courage to live a life true to myself, not the life others expected of me.** "Most people had not honored even a half of their dreams and had to die knowing that it was due to choices they had made, or not made."
2. **I wish I hadn't worked so hard.** "All of the men I nursed deeply regretted spending so much of their lives on the treadmill of a work existence."
3. **I wish I'd had the courage to express my feelings.** "They settled for a mediocre existence and never became who they were truly capable of becoming.
4. **I wish I had stayed in touch with my friends.** "Everyone misses their friends when they are dying."
5. **I wish I had let myself be happier.** "Many did not realize until the end that happiness is a choice."

Finally, according to Happify.com a number of current regrets include:

- The biggest regret of all is taking a dissatisfying job just for the money;
- 25% of homeowners have buyer's remorse.
- 29% of adults under 35 believe they have posted something that could harm their career on social media;
- 25% regret sharing selfies.
- 31% regret their tattoos.

Regret doesn't have to be something we deny or pretend never happens to us. Instead, regret can be a wake-up call where we realize we've made a decision (or two) leading us away from the peace and happiness we crave. In fact, if we are still alive and able to read this, we can begin following the expert advice that I've shared above this very minute. Learning from our regrets might not be easy, but the SMART thing to do is to allow them to redirect our lives toward greater happiness, purpose and peace.

Chapter Nine

How To Reimagine A Rightsized Life`

"Though no one can go back and make a brand new start, anyone can start from now and make a brand new ending." ~Carl Bard

Some time ago I was invited to join my first online book club through Facebook. The book to be discussed was ***Life Reimagined—Discovering Your New Life Possibilities.*** And while I was a bit skeptical about how a book club discussion through Facebook could be that helpful, this upbeat and practical book appeared to cover ideas I often read and write about—so I said yes. After completion, I consider the book club experiment to be a relative success. But best of all, I discovered along the way some helpful ideas for us all to "reimagine" what I call a rightsized life.

Once again, my definition of rightsized is a life where each of us creates an experience of life that brings us the greatest sense of well-being, peace, fulfillment and meaning. When you consider each of those elements separately it is obvious that every one of us will have a different definition of what works best. Rightsizing actually applies to every category of our lives, but it often begins when we reach a certain age.

There we begin to question what others expect of us (and maybe what we went along with for a while), and then decide that it's time to follow our own guidance and create the life we believe is possible.

Through the years, my husband Thom and I gradually rightsized our lives. Along the way we decided we didn't want, need or really desire to live up to the expectations of others. We also didn't want or need the "stuff" that our culture (and some of our neighbors) thought was that important. We instead decided that freedom, peace of mind, a focus on what matters, and a more simple and sustainable lifestyle were at the top of our list.

So what does rightsizing have to do with *Life Reimagined—Discovering Your New Life Possibilities*? In many ways they are the same. Interestingly enough, this book, which is authored by Richard J. Leider and Alan M. Webber, is also endorsed and promoted by AARP. But before any of you who are not big fans of AARP jump to conclusions (not to mention those of you who consider yourself way-ay-ay too young to be even interested), you might be as pleasantly surprised as I was by some of the insights offered in this book. One of the most profound and proactive ways it suggests we focus on our future is by beginning a conversation of "living versus aging."

Think about it. When we approach life, especially life after youth, our society normally refers to it as aging. I hear it all the time, don't you? Aging doesn't sound positive. It brings up ideas of loss, unwelcome change, and decline. But what if instead of calling it aging we merely began to recognize it as *ongoing* life. Living versus aging not only sounds more positive, it *is* more positive. Best of all, it reminds us that the entire journey of life isn't over at a certain age, it just constantly changes, adjusts and becomes something new. So while *reimagining* may focus on many who are in the second part of life, rightsizing is a similar focus on the journey of life at any age.

One of the more practical benefits of the book is a "road map and guidance system to help people navigate a new phase of life." Its "six steps to reimagining your life" is a refreshing and useful strategy that any one of us can use to steer our way through whatever change we are facing. What are the six steps?

- **Reflect.** Before any of us make any change it is wise to reflect on where we are and how we got there. The book offers several suggestions that, while not new to most of us, are great reminders for the need to be honest, open and aware with ourselves before tackling any big change.
- **Connect.** I've written about it before and the book makes it very clear—"Isolation is fatal." Those of us who plan to live a long and happy life need to stay close and connected to others.
- **Explore.** I personally loved how the book places a big emphasis on the skills of curiosity and courage no matter what our age. It points out that far too many of us have made comfort and security our primary goal in life. When we do that we sacrifice possibility and opportunity.
- **Choose.** A big part of the journey of a reimagined life is being open to possibility and then narrowing down the choices that personally bring us well-being, happiness and a sense of great possibility. And

remember, when we refuse to choose—that too is a choice.

- **Repack.** Of course before we can move too far ahead we have to let go of some of the old patterns, behaviors, people and "stuff" we've been hanging on to that no longer serve us. This step isn't easy but it is very important before we can really move forward.
- **Act.** This final step is just that—a step. It doesn't deliver us to a fully reimagined (or rightsized) life. Instead, it reminds us that it is one action followed by another, then another and another that will gradually unfold into the life we imagine. Once we complete this "act" we then return to the beginning of the map and start all over again, and again, and again.

One of the more fun things about reading this book along with others in our Facebook book discussion were comments offered by other participants. Most agreed that change isn't easy but that having a support system and hearing others talk about the process made it more doable and fun. Most seemed eager to try the map and move forward, but as might be expected, a few resisted. The book explains why that occurs by saying, "What people seem to have expected is that by the time they'd reached this point in their lives, they'd have everything under control…. What we didn't expect was that we'd have to keep figuring it out, no matter what our age." So true!

Life Reimagined is an encouraging book, but it also points out that the alternative to "living versus aging" can instead be one of limbo, resignation, and "inner kill." The book also states, "…you are responsible for shaping your own reality," and reminds us that change and "…reimagining your life is going to be messy." Ultimately, it encourages us to remember, "You are in charge of your own experiment of one."

What became increasingly clear to me as I made my way through the insights in this book was how its helpful steps can also assist us in rightsizing our lives right now. Rightsizing provides us with a perfectly tailored goal of a SMART, happy and fulfilled life. And while we will never ultimately arrive at any final destination of rightsizing, continuous reimagining helps us courageously navigate that journey in an ongoing and practical way.

Chapter Ten

Renting vs. Owning—And Other Thoughts On Impermanence

"It is not impermanence that makes us suffer. What makes us suffer is wanting things to be permanent when they are not."
~Thich Nhat Hahn

I've come to the opinion that our culture is obsessed with owning as opposed to renting. Maybe because Thom and I have a background in real estate, or because we do our best to spend time away from our home every summer when it gets really hot, a reoccurring question we're asked is, "So when are you going to buy a vacation place?" To be clear, we're not against owning property—we just prefer to rent our temporary homes instead. But it's easy to see that many people don't understand why we're perfectly happy renting and have no desire to own, regardless of how much we like the properties or enjoy the location. And that got me thinking that perhaps our culture has gotten a bit too attached to owning things and forgotten the fundamental fact that everything in life is impermanent and ultimately every *thing* is just a temporary right-to-use or leasehold estate.

Let's begin by recognizing that ownership, especially home-ownership as we know it, has only been around for a relatively short period of time in the course of human history. In hunter-gatherer societies and like most indigenous cultures that remain in the world today, it was believed that all living beings shared the land and everything upon it. Native Americans were actually shocked to discover that Europeans could "own" something that they considered a living being unto itself. Unfortunately, that belief made it very easy for those peoples to be manipulated and controlled.

Clearly, those from Europe and more industrialized and overcrowded parts of the world had discovered that whoever owned the land, controlled the land and strongly influenced anyone who lived on it. So, whether you were technically a slave or not, few were completely free when it came to land. However, in the U.S. for the first 100 to 150 years, there was so much land available that most people (at least Anglo people) felt fairly grounded and content on a plot of property. With land came the responsibility and opportunity to farm, grow your own food and create a future for yourself and your family—and that led to many individuals feeling they *owned* their land.

Then gradually, as more and more people moved to the city, farming became more industrialized and populations grew. Slowly the connections between wealth, power and land ownership grew more firmly entrenched in our culture. In an effort to develop and support a strong and healthy middle class in the U.S., the idea of home ownership was promoted and flourished during the mid-1900s and into current times. The suburbs gradually replaced individual farms. The conversion worked precisely because people longed for a sense of "place" and the relative security that a home for a lifetime provided.

Naturally, after the mid-1900s, people started learning from the rich and powerful that homes and property could be more than individual security and shelter. In a relatively short period of time, homes became an investment toward prosperity. Rather than live in a home for a lifetime, people started seeing homes as investments and mini ATMs. Meanwhile, banks and other investors recognized the money trough and began easing the rules for credit and promoting the idea of "get-rich-quick with real estate"—and soon everyone jumped on board. Surely I don't need to tell you what happened then.

With all that said, there is still another element of home ownership that is seldom realized—that is that most people don't actually OWN their home in the first place. The bank does! Even if you managed to escape the home mortgage crisis in 2007 to 2010 with a low loan-to-value mortgage—if you have *any* loan (including common area rules or association fees) against your home, you don't really own it straight out— you have partners. You may have privileges that extend beyond a leasehold, but it doesn't fully belong to you. And if you are paying more in your mortgage than what you could rent the property for, then you are going backwards, plain and simple. And never forget that the government is also your partner in every property ownership, because there are rules and conditions about what you can do on and with your property—and sometimes the government can even take it away from you.

But when it's all said and done, that still doesn't address the impermanence of ownership in the big picture. Clearly the Native Americans (and those ancient others) had the right idea. We never really *own* anything that's alive. We might control them, or break them or even kill them; but we never own their aliveness—be it a person, an animal or a planet. The essence that animates a living being is something that can't be owned.

Plus, it's important to understand that all of life is in constant flux. Everything, I mean everything changes. Anything we own today will eventually belong to someone else. Our bodies will change, our minds will change, and our relationships will change. Everything in form will be different than it is today. History is filled with dynasties and empires that have crumbled—so why should your real estate holdings (or lack thereof) be any different?

The best news of all in this is that it isn't cause for sadness and despair; quite the contrary. Instead we have reason to rejoice in the now! The only thing we can hold on to is actually what is right in front of us, right where we are, right now. The property you are sitting in, doing whatever you are doing is yours—now! The relationship you have (good or bad) is yours—now! The stuff you have accumulated is yours— now! All right now. That's it. That's all you really own in consciousness. So instead of worrying about what investments you should have made in the past, or what you hope to accomplish or own in the future, perhaps the sheer appreciation of *now* will make you the richest property owner possible.

That's why when Thom and I travel to Baja for a month and rent a condo on the beach, we are more than happy to just lease the time and experience of the place temporarily. We don't have to worry about what will happen when we leave. We can leave repairs and maintenance to the landlord and the complex, we can forget the illusion of "equity," we can walk away from a couple of the neighbors who have been less than welcoming, and we can move on to the next adventure. Sometimes, consciously renting something can be the most rewarding (and wealthy) thing possible.

Is there ever a good time to own? Of course. Not only can a home provide a wonderful sense of place to a person, it can also provide a wonderful experience of connection, plus the feeling of security and individual expression. But as I've written about before, everything is a tradeoff so every single thing you own—to an extent—owns you. That means you must not only pay for it, but maintain it as well. Whatever we claim in ownership becomes our responsibility and takes our time, resources and energy. So if a property doesn't fit consciously into our big picture, our life or our intentions, then it is probably SMART to just rent it.

Lastly, from a simple living or minimalist perspective, we need to stay conscious of a desire to purchase and own things when we don't really need them to begin with—that includes property or stuff in general. After all, most of the time when we want to buy something (anything) we are looking for a *feeling* that we think the purchase will bring us. A home to live in is particularly susceptible to this attraction. How many people end up buying a home or vacation property to *feel* proud and successful, only to have to slave at a job they hate just to pay for it and never even get to enjoy it? First identify the feeling—and then decide if there is a way to get that same feeling in a way that is more sustainable to your lifestyle. Always remember that everything you own owns *you* to a certain extent. Sometimes renting is all we need.

A leasehold is a real estate term that suggests that you have a temporary right-to-use a property. Remember—no matter how long or healthy we might live, all property ownership is really temporary. Regardless of what you believe comes after this lifetime or plane of existence—the leasehold of your life, this life, must be forfeited to embrace the next. If we celebrate what we hold right now in this moment, whether we rent or own is merely a choice. Let's make that choice as SMART as possible.

Chapter Eleven

Three Steps To Rightsize Your Work

"They deem me mad because I will not sell my days for gold; and I deem them mad because they think my days have a price." ~Kahlil Gibran

According to the online publication **Business Insider**, the average person works over 1,800 hours per year and almost 90,000 total hours during their lifetime. That might be low because if you figure 40 hours per week for 50 weeks, it comes to 2,000 hours without even counting commuting time. An even more depressing bit of information is that nearly 80% of people are dissatisfied with their jobs. So if we spend over a third of our life working and another third of our life sleeping, that leaves only one third to do everything else. Is that enough for a happy, purposeful and rewarding life? Maybe. If not, perhaps there is a better way to live by rightsizing your work in ways that help to create a SMART life 365.

Before I go very far it is probably good to define what I mean by work. While not everyone in our culture thinks of work as completely negative, a huge number of Americans dread getting up on a Monday morning to do just that.

According to the Judeo-Christian Bible, work comes after "the fall." And, for the majority of people, the ultimate goal for working 40 to 50 years is retirement. According to Salary.com, 70% of us work to live, while only 19% live to work. Clearly, work is something many of us think we have to do just to survive, rather than want to do because we can.

But work isn't all bad. We still gain benefits even if it is something we'd rather not have to do. While the basic premise is that we exchange our time for resources in order to live, work can also provide us with meaning and purpose. As Karl Pillemer, Ph.D. says in his book, **30 Lessons for Living**, work is "the way we gain a sense of self-worth and achievement, and a means of making connections with others. It is also a component of our core identity." In fact, writers at *Salary.com* believe that the ultimate goal is for us all to find a job that fulfills us both personally and professionally. But is that true?

Gary Cutting in an editorial for the **NY Times** writes, "We're ambivalent about work because in our capitalistic system it means work-for-pay (wage-labor), not for its own sake." In his article, Cutting quotes several leading philosophers who believe that the purpose of work is to give us the leisure and freedom to enjoy activities that *will* lead to greater happiness and "a good life." Unfortunately as Cutting goes on to say, "…capitalism as such is not interested in quality of life. It is essentially a system for producing things to sell at a profit, the greater the better." And in order to keep selling things, people are being raised and trained to work hard and then buy more, more and more of whatever is being sold, "regardless of its relevance to human flourishing."

The good news is that there is a way to avoid the slavery of a mechanistic and consumer culture. I call it rightsizing your work or occupation. The best thing about rightsizing is that it allows you to be in complete control of your own life, rather than blindly following the dictates of society, other people, or your own guilt or misguided expectations. Here are three ways to make the hours you spend at work (whatever that work might be), life-enhancing rather than life-depleting.

#1 Never take any job just for the money. In the book, ***30 Lessons For Living—Tried and True Advice from the Wisest Americans***, Pillemer says that the number one piece of advice offered by his interviewees in the area of work was this simple caution. After asking over 1,000 people from 65 to 100 to share their wisdom, the overwhelming consensus was that "it's vastly preferable to take home less in your paycheck and enjoy what you are doing rather than live for the weekends and your three weeks vacation a year." Pillemer calls these seniors "experts" and says, "If doing what you love requires living with less…that's a no brainer."

But the experts aren't the only ones who agree with that statement. Research study after study is showing that once our basic needs are met, we won't be any happier working harder or making more money. Daniel Gilbert, professor of psychology at Harvard University, wrote a book about it, and popular career coach Penelope Trunk insists, "More money does not make more happiness." Ultimately, as Richard Easterlin, professor of economics at the University of Southern California says, "How much pleasure people get from their job is independent of how much it pays."

But why don't more of us get this message? What parent would encourage their child to be a prostitute or a drug dealer for the money? What wife or husband would ask their partner to sell their soul just for a bigger paycheck? Yet isn't that what any of us do if we encourage those we love to work at jobs they hate just so we can buy more stuff? Until we are willing to give a happy and fulfilling life a higher priority than the money that any job generates, this will not change.

#2 Find a job that fulfills you and makes you happy. Seek and find a job that fits your personality, talents and life goals— and never lose faith that one is out there. The good news is that many younger people today are holding out for fulfilling jobs and switching when it makes sense. In older generations, far too many stuck it out in dead end jobs they hated for their entire lives, just to bring home the money. As Pillemer's "experts" suggest, "the tragedy isn't finding ourselves in the wrong job; it's staying there."

Over and over these experts of advancing age reported that even when it was extremely challenging, finding something you love to do was still the best way to experience a happy life. Overwhelmingly they believe we all spend way too much of our short lifetimes working to ever stay stuck in jobs we hate.

Of course the "experts" were also quick to say that if you find yourself in a job that isn't completely satisfying, part of the responsibility to make it rewarding falls on your shoulders. They were adamant that we should see work challenges as "learning experiences and to take advantage of any opportunity to gather knowledge about an industry or occupation."

Another primary key to making a job something that fulfills a person and provides meaning is to seek "autonomy" as much as possible. Because autonomy is one of the most important attributes of a satisfying occupation, finding ways to act on one's own as much as possible usually leads to greater happiness. That's why becoming self-employed, regardless of the amount of money to be made, is usually so desirable.

#3 Learn to think of money as something you trade for your "life energy" and time. This powerful idea was made popular by the book ***Your Money Or Your Life*** written by Joe Dominguez and Vicki Robin in 1992. This book recommends that people become extremely clear about exactly how much they have, how much they make, and *precisely* how much time they trade to get that money. Ninety-nine times out of 100, people will discover that the time they spend working (and getting ready to work, traveling to work, and coming home from work) absorbs far more of their life energy than they realize. That's when the book offers 101 tips to help people learn to make changes, prioritize their time, and spend their money more efficiently for maximum enjoyment.

While this might seem to be a strange strategy to rightsize your work, I think it's critical for us each to closely examine and recognize how valuable our time and "life energy" is. Most of us will admit that time is more precious than money but our lives often don't reflect that truth. Only after we become more aware can we make better choices every single day.

Another suggestion in the book ***Your Money or Your Life*** is to ask ourselves three basic and timeless questions about our work and our lives to stay on track:

1. Do I receive fulfillment, satisfaction and value in proportion to life energy spent?
2. Is this expenditure of life energy in alignment with my values and life purpose?
3. How might this expenditure change if I didn't have to work for a living?

So while there are a lot more suggestions I could offer to explain how to rightsize your work, until the above three ideas are addressed, any others are only band-aids for an overall chronic condition. Fortunately, my husband Thom and I both feel the same way about work and making it a focus—so yes, our work is rightsized for us. Not only do we have a profoundly happy and content life, we don't struggle for money like we did when we were younger. Once we incorporated the above questions into both our actions and our perceptions, the rest followed.

If work takes up so much of our lives, then we all owe it to ourselves to make that time and experience as meaningful, fulfilling and yes, as happy as possible. We owe that to our partners and our children as well. The "experts" in Pillemer's books all agreed saying, "There's no harsher penalty than to wake up and go to work at a job you don't like." By consistently stopping and asking ourselves, "what is most important and where do we want to spend our precious time, talents and life energy", we are guided to a path that is both happy and SMART, 365.

Chapter Twelve

How To Feel Rich, Safe & Content—No Matter What

"It is better to live rich than to die rich." ~Samuel Johnson

In case you're wondering, this chapter is not about getting rich or making money. It is also not about the latest in security technology or the suggestion that you should be happy just the way you are. Instead, I want to explore the biggest obstacle to why most of us don't really *feel* rich, safe or content regardless of how much money we have in the bank, the circumstances surrounding us, or how great things might be at any point. That big "elephant in the room" is an underlying, all-pervasive and largely unconscious belief in scarcity. In fact, whether you are on the path to a simple or minimalist lifestyle, trying to rightsize your life or just getting by as you are—I'm convinced that uncovering our true feelings about scarcity is one of the most important steps we can ever take to increase our individual well being. Interested?

The insidious nature of a scarcity mindset was recently brought back to my attention by author Brene Brown in her book, ***Daring Greatly***. While I had previously been aware of ideas of scarcity from a financial perspective, Brown suggests that a major component of most of the problems in the entire world stem from this all-encompassing fear-based mentality of "never enough." As Brown says, "Scarcity thrives in a culture where everyone is hyperaware of lack. Everything from safety and love to money and resources feels restricted or lacking. We spend inordinate amounts of time calculating how much we have, want, and don't have, and how much everyone else has, needs and wants." Unfortunately, constantly focusing on "not-enoughness" challenges our sense of vulnerability and triggers our shame. That is largely why Brown is convinced that scarcity is at the root of all of our feelings of shame, comparison and disengagement. And that of course is why most of us don't feel rich, safe or content in spite of how good our lives are.

Brown isn't the first person to speak out about the problems of scarcity or "lack thinking." Author Lynne Twist in her book, **The Soul of Money** offers this classic explanation of the issue:

> For me, and for many of us, our first waking thought of the day is, I didn't get enough sleep. The next one is "I don't have enough time." Whether true or not, that thought of not-enough occurs to us automatically before we even think to question or examine it. We spend most of the hours and the days of our lives hearing, explaining, complaining, or worrying about what we don't have enough of….Before we even sit up in bed, before our feet touch the floor, we're already inadequate, already behind, already losing,

already lacking something. And by the time we go to bed at night, our minds are racing with a litany of what we didn't get, or didn't get done, that day. We go to sleep burdened by those thoughts and wake up to that reverie of lack...This internal condition of scarcity, this mind-set of scarcity, lives at the very heart of our jealousies, our greed, our prejudice, and our arguments with life...

Once we see it from this clear perspective, it is easy to see that scarcity has most of us in its grip—not to mention entire countries and their leaders. While it is easy to point fingers at those in our world who are acting from fear or greed, an awareness of how deep this consciousness of scarcity lives in *each of us* is needed. Anytime I compare myself unfavorably to anyone else, every time I am fearful of anything, anytime I'm worried about something—at the core of every one of those situations I am putting my faith and belief in the idea of scarcity. And when I do, how can I ever be enough, how could I ever *have* enough—to feel rich, safe and content?

I find Brown's perspective on scarcity so compelling because, as she says, "Worrying about scarcity is our culture's version of post traumatic stress...and rather than coming together to heal (which requires vulnerability), we're angry and scared and at each other's throats." Brown is convinced that this climate of scarcity influences our culture in three major ways. Those ways are:

1. **Shame:** We ridicule and belittle others as a way to control or keep people in line. We control ourselves by tying our self-worth to achievement, productivity, compliance and even perfectionism.

2. **Comparison:** We constantly compare and rank others and ourselves, holding each to a narrow standard or ideal. Creativity is stifled and ignored.
3. **Disengagement:** We all disconnect to avoid judgment or to remain unseen. We refuse to listen or pay attention and feel no one is listening or paying attention to us. We avoid trying anything new or taking risks.

So what's the solution? According to Brown it begins by saying, "The opposite of 'never enough' isn't abundance or 'more than you could ever imagine.' The opposite of scarcity is (simply) *enough...*" She believes that the way to overcome such thinking is to cultivate what she calls "Wholeheartedness." A wholehearted person is someone who lives their life courageously, "facing uncertainty, exposure, and emotional risks" all the time holding a deep belief that they are enough and the world itself is enough, exactly as it is.

Twist offers this suggestion by saying, "You have to recognize that you're swimming in the lie. Because when you're chasing *more* so obsessively, you can't see 'enough' – it doesn't even exist for you. The radical truth is there is enough right now, right this minute...when you let go of trying to get more of what you don't really need... it frees up oceans of energy to pay attention to and make a difference with what you already have. I like to say, 'What you appreciate appreciates.' What you already have grows in the nourishment of your attention and intention."

Twist goes on to say that this "enoughness" is actually an awareness of "sufficiency." But she is also clear that sufficiency isn't "two steps up from poverty or one step short of abundance." Instead, sufficiency isn't an amount at all. "It is an experience, a context we generate, a declaration, a knowing there is enough, and that we are enough."

Ultimately it may not matter how "minimal" you live, how few pieces of clothing or furniture you own, or whether you live in a tiny house or a mansion. Regardless of whether we have a billion bucks in the bank or $10 in our wallet, if any of us continue to let scarcity rule our lives it will never be enough. I agree with both Twist and Brown when they say that we must counteract the consciousness of scarcity with an ongoing awareness and internal work to turn such thinking around. Brown admits that she and her husband work every single day to overcome "the cultural norms driven by scarcity," and that it takes courage and vulnerability "every time we make choices that challenge the social climate of scarcity." Only when we wholeheartedly embrace sufficiency consciousness can we ever live completely rich, safe and content—no matter what.

Chapter Thirteen

Rightsizing Your Finances—A SMART Way To Manage Money

"Fear about how one will support oneself in the future arises not because there is no way of sustaining oneself, but because one's mind is poor."
~Jae Woong Kim

A couple of weeks ago, my husband Thom and I got into a discussion about rightsizing while talking with friends during happy hour. I could tell that even though everyone agreed that going debt free was a wonderful element of rightsizing and simple living, most felt it was out of reach for the average family. That was a great reminder that rightsizing isn't just about the size of your house, your car, or your credit limit—instead, rightsizing touches every area of your life including (and maybe especially) your finances. In fact, once a person learns to manage their money—both expenses and income—rightsizing the other areas of life will come more easily. Down the line, a person can eventually achieve the ultimate goal of rightsizing, which is to live a life that uniquely fits and brings the greatest amount of peace, contentment and joy to that individual and family.

The good news, or the bad news depending upon your perspective, is that there is no money formula for you to follow to rightsize your finances. No one, me included, can tell you how much you need to live a life that will bring you contentment, peace and joy. There are about a gazillion stories on the internet from people around the world who get by on practically no income whatsoever, but who live amazing lives. On the other hand, there are plenty of other stories about people deeply in debt with an income of $400,000+ per year. Rightsizing doesn't judge, but it does ask us to be responsible for what we say we need, pay our way as we go, and be very clear about what we will (or won't) do with our finances.

With that said, there are guidelines that might be helpful. A few ***expense strategies*** are:

1) Live *below* your means. If you make a practice of spending less than what you actually have coming in, you'll have extra money to save and spend should a special need arise. Unfortunately our culture teaches us to spend as much as we make as though that were a reward for working hard. The untold secret is how great it feels to know you can easily pay your bills and even have extra money available for expected surprises.

2) Don't spend money that you don't have. The big one in this category is remembering that credit is not the same as money—it's credit. Sure it might be fun to indulge yourself by spending money you don't actually have on a splurge—but when debt is hanging over our heads and we have no way to repay it, it is very difficult to live a happy and stress free life.

Many years ago Thom and I actually lived on our credit cards for a time and ended up with over $40,000 in debt. That obligation took years to pay off and drained our lives of enthusiasm and peace of mind. The huge amount of interest we were required to pay each month just to make minimum payments was more than a mortgage payment. Debt sucks the life out of you, and I've heard it said that every time you spend money you don't have (using things like credit cards), or sign on the dotted line for a house or car you don't actually need, you are shackling yourself to a ball and chain for the next ___ number of years. The good news is that it is possible, with focus and discipline, to pay off the worst of your debt.

3) Sometimes it is better to rent than buy. Our culture is obsessed with owning things, so much so that many people find themselves shelling out the money to buy toys and other luxuries that they could (and probably should) rent. While it might be nice to tell everyone you own that second home in an exotic location, please consider what it will cost sitting there vacant when you aren't using it. Or think about how many times you might actually use that motor home/camper/trailer/boat before you shell out the money to buy it! We don't have to own things to enjoy them—sometimes renting or even sharing is a better solution.

4) Be careful about thinking of your purchases as an "investment." Investing for the future can be very profitable. Unfortunately, far too many people purchase items and call them investments rather than buying something that actually generates income. FYI…. cars, boats, time-shares, art and even a home are not investments. Unless a purchase brings income into your household, it is really just another expense—there is a difference and we should know that.

5) Be very honest with yourself about what you really need to be happy. I was talking with a girlfriend recently (yes you know who you are!) and she told me that she didn't have room in her large walk-in closet for all her clothes and shoes. When I suggested a good solution would be to give some away she told me she already had given *a lot* away, but really *needed* everything else. Really? That same argument came up again recently with a family member who told us he really *needed* that expensive car with its payment of $700+ per month to impress clients. Really? Instead, if you are serious about the benefits of rightsizing your finances I suggest you honestly look at what you think you need and the excuses you tell yourself.

Of course, if you believe you really need that house, that car, those clothes or whatever, and are willing to pay for the consequences of having them, then that is definitely your choice. The biggest problem I see with buying extravagant things that we say we need is that psychological studies prove that very shortly after buying those items the pleasure received diminishes rapidly. Plus, as I mentioned in the case of my girlfriend, owning that pleasure becomes an extra burden that must be handled. Everything we buy and then own carries a price and responsibility. But rather than analyze the cost and commitment, many people continue to tell themselves they need those items instead of admitting they've been pursuing the wrong dream the entire time.

A few ***income strategies*** for rightsizing are:

1) Avoid doing anything just for the money. While most people will righteously say they would never prostitute themselves, a huge number will take on jobs they dislike for no other reason than the money it brings them. Unfortunately, most of us don't value our time, talents and creativity enough, so we squander them for a few dollars just to buy stuff that we often don't even need. Worse yet, we insist others we know and love (husbands, wives, children, etc.) do the same. On the other hand, rightsizing suggests that we focus our talents and passions on those things that hold value for others and ourselves. We then let go of making money the goal, and instead make work a gift we offer the world.

2) Do what you love and the money will follow. During my life this principle has played itself out over and over. I became a writer not because I had any training or education in it, and certainly not because I thought it would generate a lot of income, but because it was something that I dreamed of doing. Want to know whether you love what you do? Just ask yourself if you would do it even if you won a $10 million lottery. If you aren't working at something that makes your heart sing and your feet jump out of bed in the morning, then it might be time to look for something different. In the end everything has a price—including our work. If we are just putting in time doing something we dislike—we might be making money but there is always additional cost to our activity. If we work at something we love—then the joy of that is bringing in far, far more than the money we deposit in the bank.

3) The limits or caps on our income are there because *we* put them there. Many years ago, Thom and I had a teacher named Dr. Tom Costa. Many of the people he taught were older and retired and I can clearly remember Dr. Tom telling those people, "The only one who 'fixes' your income is you." Naturally, many of the audience would argue saying that they had to exist on a fixed social security check each month. At that, Dr. Tom reminded them that there was a huge abundant universe all around them and they were the ones who were choosing to live merely on their social security.

From a spiritual perspective the concepts of "like attracts like", "what you think about you bring about," "it is done unto you as you believe" and many other statements suggest that we are the ones who decide how much we can accept and receive in our lives—financially and otherwise. During the first half of our married life, Thom and I found it very difficult to rise above the income levels of our family-of-origin. But by working on our consciousness and our ability to accept and receive, we have risen to an income level that is far beyond our previous expectations. Whether or not you believe in a spiritual aspect to income and intentionality is entirely your choice.

4) Retirement is overrated. Most people who crave retirement are working at jobs they dislike or have grown tired of doing. Rather than take a chance and live a life of passion today, they delay it for a promise that may or may not ever arrive. Instead, if we pursue a job that brings us happiness, contentment and joy every single day then we don't have to concern ourselves with how or when to retire. If we all focused on doing jobs we loved that produced help and service for others, then every day for the rest of our lives would be filled with meaning and purpose. Who would want to retire from that?

5) Rightsizing our income is all about balance. Which would you rather be?

A) A person who makes a good amount of money from work he/she enjoys and then shares it with those they love, along with plenty of downtime to relax, enjoy or create; or,
B) A person who makes an enormous amount of money at a job that is highly stressful and requires long and grueling hours so that that there is little time to spend with those he/she loves and even less time to relax, enjoy or create.

Of course, the choice isn't usually that obvious and is seldom either/or. But my point is that everything comes at a responsibility or cost—be it time, energy or spiritual coin. We alone decide what works for us, and when we find what makes our heart sing and also allows us to sleep well at night, then chances are good we have rightsized our income stream.

Keep in mind that rightsizing is finding a lifestyle that brings *you* the greatest amount of peace and happiness. What works for me might not work for anyone else. But in order for it to succeed, each of us must spend time and reflection discovering it for ourselves—and then implementing it in our day-to-day life. While I believe my guidelines to be universal, there's a chance that they barely touch on what needs to happen in your life to live your peaceful and happy existence. Beginning the conversation about what is important to you, what brings you joy, what stresses you out and what gives your life purpose, freedom and meaning, will all help point the way to rightsizing your finances. Is it worth it? Trust me—this is an investment that will prove worthy of your time.

Chapter Fourteen

Packing Light & Other Thoughts on Eliminating The Unnecessary

> *"He who would travel happily must travel light."*
> ~Antoine de St. Exupery

After nearly a dozen overseas trips I've learned that you really don't need to take as much stuff as you think you do. In so many ways, that also offers us all a lesson in rightsizing. Of course it is easier for guys because they can get away with a pair of jeans and a couple of t-shirts. But even though I'm responsible for toiletries and toothbrushes, I've learned that the penalty for lugging around a ton of stuff while trying to enjoy yourself is not worth the benefit of having it "just in case you need it." And that made me think about all the other things I've tried to over-pack throughout the years, and a few things I've discovered about eliminating unnecessary clutter.

Part of the problem is that as we get older we start expecting more comfort. When I was younger, I didn't mind sleeping in the car on the way to somewhere if I didn't have the money for a motel. I've even slept in a tent, although I've never been much of a camper. At the time, a cheap picnic or fast food was a perfectly acceptable way to eat dinner. But gradually through the years Thom and I got more and more accustomed to king-sized beds in hotels with air conditioning and restaurants that served fresh and nutritious entrees. And did I mention how nice it is to fly business class? So after a while the temptation is to adjust your adventures to fit the circumstances that you find most comfortable. That can easily lead to spending more money than necessary—as well as the danger of insulating yourself from some of the most rewarding aspects of travel in the first place by dragging along too much stuff.

So, keeping in mind that the goal of travel (just like the goal of life) is to enjoy the journey as much as the destination, here are a few things I've learned along the way about letting go of the unnecessary:

* **Experiencing every part of the trip is as important as arriving at the ultimate destination.** I used to think of travel as just the means to getting where I wanted to be. Unfortunately, that kind of thinking is epidemic in our culture and we end up sacrificing so much along the way just to reach what we think will make us happy. When travelling, I routinely see people at the airports so loaded down with luggage and paraphernalia that they are struggling to move. Being casual and relaxed, and having only a few pieces of luggage to mind in transit, allows you to sit back and enjoy even a busy airport— not to mention a busy life.

* **The more stuff you take with you the more you have to manage along the way.** While I consider my laptop as important as my toothbrush, it does come with some

88

responsibility. Clothes are the same—instead, when you make certain your few pieces of wardrobe go together, it takes the guesswork out of what to wear. Every single item we take with us fills up our time and attention, so let's make sure that we take only those things that hold importance. It's not so much what you take, as your willingness to accept the trade-off of having it along.

* **Never forget how the Peak-End rule affects your memory.** In case you've forgotten, this cognitive process suggests that most of the time people remember the PEAKS of their vacation along with the ending, far more than they will remember all the rest of the details. For example, the "peak" will usually be a strong emotional response to some event, either good or bad, that happened during the trip. The end will be the overall feelings about how the trip ended. The way our memories work, soon after we return from our trip those two elements—the peak and the ending—will be what we remember.

With that in mind, it makes sense to include several "peaks" that will stick out long after you return and to plan something special in the end. And, if that's mostly what we remember long into the future, why make ourselves crazy planning amazing (and likely expensive) activities along the way? In fact, too many activities will soon be forgotten and are unnecessary for a happy experience overall. Then add in the experience of dragging along too much stuff, and your memory of the trip will be one of struggle rather than fun.

* **Relationships are always more important than stuff.** Who we go with and those we meet along the way will

often affect our travels more than our destination. I still remember very vividly a great dinner conversation with two young men Thom and I met in a smoky pub in Edinburgh nearly ten years ago, shortly after the invasion of Iraq. The men were from a university in Spain and only partially spoke English—but their warmth and intelligence made several hours pass very quickly and enjoyably.

I also remember another trip travelling with another couple who had dramatically different touring styles than Thom and me. We both learned from that experience to be very careful about our travelling companions in the future. Because people have the ability to affect our emotions so dramatically, it's important to remember that the people you encounter along the way will make the "peaks" of your vacation, and your life, stand out.

* There is no way I could ever take enough stuff with me to make me feel safe if I don't already have that mindset. Unfortunately, I think many of us take so much with us when we travel (or experience life) because it makes us feel more safe and secure. If I take that special pillow, then I'm convinced I'll sleep better. If I take that extra pair of shoes, my feet won't hurt. If I pack that cold medicine, I'll have what I need if I get sick. And never forget Pepto-Bismol!

So instead of feeling confident that we can handle any eventuality, we pretend we can shield ourselves from those events. As one of my most favorite quotes from Helen Keller goes, "Security is mostly a superstition. It does not exist in nature, nor do the children of men as a whole experience it.

Avoiding danger is no safer in the long run than outright exposure. Life is either a daring adventure, or nothing."

* Clutter in your head can ruin a good vacation as much as too much luggage. Ever gone on a trip when you're worried or distracted by a major concern? Sometimes the most cluttered part of our lives is our mind. It may not be easy, but attempting to let go of worries or problems before you leave might be one of the best things you can do to have a good trip.

* We need far, far less than we think we need. One of the best things about travel is the very real experience of how little we need to experience and appreciate life. After living out of a suitcase for several weeks it feels decadent to come home to a closet filled with clothes, a pantry full of food, and a house full of stuff. Again, I think most of the items we accumulate in our lives are dedicated to the pursuit of comfort and security. While those are not necessarily bad, if they hold us back from experiencing the sweet nectar of life, then they become a crutch rather than an aid.

Consumption and clutter are very real obstacles to happiness that can often be avoided with greater awareness both at home or on the road. So, regardless of whether you are planning a trip any time soon or looking to rightsize your entire life, it might be SMART to take a good hard look at the baggage we all carry around with us every single day and decide if it's worth taking along.

Chapter Fifteen

A Variation On A Bucket List—The F^k It List!*

"We must be willing to let go of the life we've planned, so as to have the life that is waiting for us." ~Joseph Campbell

A couple of weeks ago Thom and I had lunch with a long-time friend I'll call Bob. After a great meal our conversation turned to health and successful aging as it sometimes does for people in midlife. We all agreed that we were extremely fortunate to live in an area where we can observe people well into their 90's who are vibrant, active and younger in mind and heart than many people half their age.

Next we talked about the importance of living each day as a gift, never taking a moment for granted, and fulfilling our bucket list while we were all healthy and financially able. That's when Bob joked that he recently had dinner with a woman in her late 80's who had a different take on the idea. She told him very emphatically that she was done with the idea of a bucket list. At her age, she was working on her F*^k It list! And while we all laughed at the spunk of Bob's friend, that declaration got me thinking.

Sure, it's healthy to have a bucket list containing all the goals and dreams we hope to accomplish during the remainder of our lives. But maybe a F*^k It list is good as well. After all, at a certain age we should be both willing and able to let go of ANYTHING that drags us down and holds us back from living a happy and content life. So, after some time thinking about it—here are a few things I'm putting on my F*^k It list that perhaps might convince some of the rest of you to make such a list as well.

The very first thing on my F*^k It list is caring what others think about me. I've cared about that for far too long, and it's time to just say "F*^k It!" Of course, even as I write this I'm aware that I don't normally use four-letter-words, so writing this post with f*^k in the title (and in the text!) is quite a step for me. But again, it's all because I worry too much about whether you, my friends and my readers will like it. Most of the time I find plenty of other words that work equally as well or better. But let's face it—sometimes f*^k is just the right word, and right now, I'm giving myself permission to use it when it seems to fit the circumstance.

Second is giving up the need/desire to have people like me. Again, this is something I've carried around for most of my life, and it's time to just say "F*^k It!" I know, and you probably do too, that not everyone likes everyone else for all sorts of reasons. You might not like my politics, my sense of humor, my take-charge attitude or any one of dozens of characteristics that I have—and that's okay. Just like not everyone likes chocolate, not everyone will like me either. So instead of trying to make myself into someone that everyone might like—I'm going to focus on those people who like me just as I am and appreciate what I uniquely offer the world. And maybe, just maybe, when I give myself permission to just be myself regardless of whether it rubs people the wrong way or the right way—I will give others permission to be themselves as well.

Next I say "F*^k It!" to ever listening to trolls and/or other critics in relationship to my writing. Maybe because I've had no formal training or a related degree—or maybe because it's always been so important to me, for whatever the reason I've always been sensitive about my writing. True, it's gotten better as I go along because I've been doing it so long, but I still care more than I should about how some people judge my writing. And in spite of the fact that I've now got a number of people reading my blog who seem to appreciate both my style and my variety of topics, I sometimes catch myself paying more attention to the critics than I do to my fans. And it's time to say "F*^k It" to listening to trolls. As author Brene Brown says, "…I can't be paralyzed anymore by the critics. My new mantra is, if you're not in the arena getting your ass kicked on occasion, then I'm not interested in your feedback."

Plus, I think it's time for me to definitely say "F*^k It" to whether or not I look attractive or "good for my age." For the most part, I don't obsess about my looks or my clothing. (Those who know me personally can likely attest to that!) But what I've noticed at this age is that there is a very strong emphasis on us all, especially women, to look younger than we supposedly should and do anything and everything we should to stay there. While I'm all for feeling energetic and vibrant— and good health is very important to me, I say "F*^k It!" to trying to please other people's definition of what my age should look like, act like, or be.

The last thing that I think it's high time to say "F*^k It!" to is fear. Yep, I'm going out on a limb here by saying that I'll bet I'm not the only one who could let this one go and be happier. Remember, most of the time fear isn't real—instead it's 'False Evidence Appearing Real.' Or as Dale Carnegie said, "You can conquer almost any fear if you will only make up your mind to do so. For remember, fear doesn't exist anywhere except in the mind." But fear tends to be tricky and disguise itself in all sorts of ways and means. For example, I might not think that I'm afraid of what others think, but if I insist on perfectionism, then I am holding myself back from a fear of not being good enough. Fear is anything that consciously or unconsciously keeps us from enjoying, appreciating and loving every moment of our lives. And I say "F*^k it!" to anything that does that!

Okay, I think I've given you enough to get the point. I realize after writing this that I've only touched the surface of things I should finally let go of and say "F*^K It!" to in my life. Chances are good that my list will keep growing from here on out. But now that I've raised the idea, I suggest that you spend some time allowing the idea to soak into your head and see if there isn't something you'd like to do the same with as well. SMART Living or rightsizing isn't always about doing something or adding something to your life to make it better. Sometimes the best course of action is letting something go and to just say, "F*^k It!"

Chapter Sixteen

Rightsizing: Choosing Semi-Retirement Instead of Retired

"If you love what you do you will never work a day in your life."
~Confucius

A good friend of mine plans to retire in the next couple of months. She's earned it. After working at a challenging job for over 25 years, she's more than ready to move on to something new. But underlying that excitement I detected a bit of worry about the uncertainty before her. That mixed message of elation and concern got me thinking about how Thom and I are approaching our future. What I realized was that in our quest to rightsize our lives, Thom and I have gradually slipped into what we are calling semi-retirement in a natural and stress-free way. While so many people our age are asking an all-or-nothing question about retirement, rightsizing right now might be the best solution of all.

Is All-or-Nothing Retirement Outdated?

Let's face it, the old model of working at a 9 to 5 job for 25 to 40 years and then retiring isn't an option for most people any more. Unless we work in the public sector (government), we can't count on a company having our back. Hoping and dreaming for a gold watch and a pension are things of the past. Unfortunately, I've talked to many who are still stuck in that old dream of ending work and never working another day in their life.

In addition, the old model of slaving it out at a job we don't like is also in question. Do we really want to be as Emile Gauvreau says, "I was part of a strange race of people aptly described as spending their lives doing things they detest, to make money they don't want, to buy things they don't need, to impress people they don't like"? And with reports from the Bureau of Labor Statistics saying that Americans average 11 jobs during a lifetime, why would we stick it out at something we hate if there are other options?

The final issue that can't be ignored is that many people will simply not be able to financially retire—ever. As massive amounts of baby boomers enter retirement age every single day, the AP-NORC Center for Public Affairs Research survey says, "Thirty-nine percent of workers age 50 and older report having $100,000 or less saved for retirement, not including pensions or homes; and 24 percent have less than $10,000." With so little in savings, and nothing but Social Security as guaranteed income, most seniors must continue working as long as they are physically able.

Why Do We Want to Retire Anyway?

Of course, maybe the real question is why we want to retire in the first place. Chances are it's about control.

According to an article in the Canadian Journal **FINANCIAL POST**, "The real key is being in control. How else to explain that the average retirement age for the self-employed in Canada is 69...By contrast, workers who are employed by someone else retire at age 62, on average. They wouldn't leave so early if they were motivated by their jobs, but most of them have little control over what they do or how they do it." I'll bet many in the U.S. over age 50 feel the same. It's not that people don't want to keep contributing and staying active, but they do want to have some level of control over the work and the hours. It's likely that most people don't want to retire and DO NOTHING; most of us just want to stop doing work that makes us unhappy.

That's where rightsizing fits in. A simple definition of rightsizing is designing and living a particular lifestyle that allows you to focus on the things in life that really matter. It's eliminating the should's, the have-to's and the rules that we've allowed society to use to box us in, and to instead reinvent our own world. Because I've written about it so much I recently realized how similar rightsizing and semi-retirement look from the outside. Most of us want to believe we are in charge of our lives and rightsizing allows us to create it from the inside out.

What's the Solution?

So where do we start? If we are like my friend and just a couple of years from a set retirement, we might want to stay the course. Then once we officially retire, we can reanalyze what it is that will bring us the most joy and do that. But for any of us in work that feels unsatisfying, unfulfilling and beyond our control, maybe it's time to start looking for a new way to live. And before we complain that we can't because of the money, let's start being very honest about what we are willing to sell our souls for in return. When asked directly, I doubt there are any of us that will admit that we will do ANYTHING for money. So if that's true, by recognizing that we've used the "money excuse" as a reason to hold ourselves back from living a peaceful and satisfying existence, we just might finally give ourselves permission to find something else. If we can't do something else, maybe we find a way to reinvent how we are doing what we do. Fewer hours? Different department? There are ALWAYS options.

Of course, rightsizing isn't just about working or not working. Rightsizing is about eliminating the unessential and focusing on what really matters. Author Greg McKeown says it over and over in his book, ***ESSENTIALISM—THE DISCIPLINED PURSUIT OF LESS*** when he asks, "What if we stopped celebrating being busy as a measurement of importance? What if instead we celebrated how much time we had spent listening, pondering, meditating, and enjoying time with the most important people in our lives? What if the whole world shifted from the undisciplined pursuit of more to the disciplined pursuit of less…only better?"

Once we start rightsizing our lives, we let go of comparing ourselves to the lives of others and needing or even wanting a bunch of stuff to define us. When we don't spend all that money buying things we don't really need, we often find we don't require nearly as much money as we thought we did. That's when we can stop working so much, or give up work that sucks the joy out of us. As we start being picky about where we spend our time, and eliminate wasteful spending, we easily slide into a rightsized semi-retirement.

There is nothing wrong with wanting to slow down and enjoy our lives as we age. But I think it is possible to start doing that sooner rather than later by rightsizing our lives right now. Besides, there will never be a time when we don't have something valuable to contribute to the world in terms of our experience and wisdom, it is just having the awareness to choose when, where and how we will share it in ways that will be most rewarding. Thom and I don't ever plan to retire, but thanks to rightsizing, we are living and enjoying the many benefits of semi-retirement right now. So no matter where each of us is on the journey of life, rightsizing your life just might be a SMART solution to where you go from here.

Chapter Seventeen

7 Signs of Real Abundance

> *"Abundance is about being rich, with or without money."*
> ~Suze Orman

My husband Thom and I recently spent some time talking with a young couple we know about the direction of their life. With one small child and hope for one more, they are considering moving to a larger home to give them all more space in a slightly more prestigious neighborhood. That certainly means larger mortgage payments, higher utility costs, more stuff, and a longer commute. Still, they seem convinced it would all be worth it. After all, isn't that the American Dream—more, bigger, better? Thom and I kept our mouths shut because they appeared to want encouragement more than advice. Yet because I wish someone had tried to explain to a younger me that the dream we sought was not really a bigger house or more stuff, I thought I'd share what the joy of real abundance has come to mean to me after all these years.

Along the way, I've learned that real abundance has nothing to do with cash in the bank. It has nothing to do with expensive houses, cars or technology. There's also no connection to fame, adulation and fortune, although there's no rule against it. Instead, the approach to abundance that I'm learning to live by, more and more as life goes on, is one where I recognize and trust my connection and alignment with a benevolent Universe. Even if that doesn't make much sense to you, just know that real abundance has nothing whatsoever to do with any feelings of fear, scarcity, lack or not-enoughness.

In fact, if you are feeling fear about your life, distrust of the Universe, or that there is never, ever enough of what you need to be happy and at peace, then no amount of money or stuff will make you feel real abundance. As Laurence Boldt says in his book, **THE TAO OF ABUNDANCE**, "…for most of us, the feeling of lack is not a result of a lack of things or material stuff. It is a sense of struggle and a lack of ease; a lack of energy; a feeling of powerlessness and blocked expression; a lack of harmony and connection in relationship; a lack of time to be, grow and relate; and a lack of opportunity to fully appreciate and celebrate the beauty in life—that gives a sense of deficiency to our existence."

With that in mind, here are my seven signs that show what it's like to live in real abundance:

1) Regularly enjoying a luxury of time. I know lots of people who have a lot more money than I do, but often when I ask them about their lives, they are too busy to enjoy it. I'll bet you do too. In our culture there is an obsession with working hard to prove our success. Unfortunately, even when you are successful you worry that you have to work even harder or you'll lose it all. Many slave away at jobs they detest for 20 to 30 years just so they can finally retire and enjoy themselves.

In contrast, Boldt says, "For the Taoists, leisure is the ESSENCE of abundance." Anyone who doesn't know how to take time to relax and regularly do nothing is firmly in the grasp of a scarcity mentality. Real luxury is not working like a maniac to take an expensive vacation—it is living a life you enjoy every day. Real abundance is embracing the moments of today as a precious gift filled with 24 hours that will never be repeated.

2) Freedom to navigate the course of our days. During our early-married life, I struggled with the idea that Thom and I didn't fit the mold of what I THOUGHT defined success. Neither of us had a college degree or a prestigious occupation. There was no corporate ladder to climb even if we'd found one lying around. Instead, what I've since discovered is that our decision to be entrepreneurial was one of the greatest gifts we could give ourselves. It gave us the freedom to try out several paths that captured our interest. It allowed us to use our imagination to create opportunities where none existed before. Best of all, it gave us the freedom to live life doing what we love and to make choices based on the calling of our hearts.

3) Peace of mind. One of the easiest ways to spot someone who lives with a scarcity mentality is to listen to their conversations. Most of their talk is filled with fear, doubt and uncertainty about the economy, the government, their jobs, the future and just about everything else. In contrast, Boldt says, "To live in abundance is to be fully alive, free of any sense of lack or desperation."

Boldt offers a cute story about a man who leaves his small village and travels the world. When he returns, all the people of the village rush around him asking, "How is life out in the world?" The man says simply, "Same as here. It is good for those who know how to live."

4) Living with meaning and purpose. Anyone who believes that their daily work is a calling, with an awareness of their unique purpose and meaning, lives abundantly every day. As Katharine Graham, former owner and publisher of the Washington Post said, "To love what you do and feel that it matters—how could anything be more fun?"

5) Deep connections to others. There are currently dozens of scientific studies, books and research papers that prove that those who are happiest and live longest are those with supportive, loving and long-lasting relationships—partners, friends and community. Cultivating, protecting and honoring our relationships are keys to the priceless feeling of abundance in our lives.

6) An understanding of our place in the Universe.
According to Boldt, the Taoists believe, "If you put yourself in accord with the way of the universe, it will take care of you abundantly." While your view of your place in the Universe might be different than mine, as long as you rest in the belief of a loving and benevolent Source-Of-Being that wants good for you, you will experience a life of real abundance.

7) Deep gratitude for all the good you have. As author Melody Beattie says, "Gratitude unlocks the fullness of life. It turns what we have into enough, and more. It turns denial into acceptance, chaos into order, confusion into clarity. It can turn a meal into a feast, a house into a home, a stranger into a friend. Gratitude makes sense of our past, brings peace for today, and creates a vision for tomorrow."

When you think about it, anyone who spends the hours of their days chasing after money, fame or power is really just a slave to the belief that there is only so much to go around. On the other hand, when we start recognizing the incredible abundance that makes up the world, we can start seeing ourselves surrounded by an abundance of love, creativity, ideas, opportunities, awareness, friends, beauty, happiness, fun and so, so much more.

I'm not sure what direction our young friends will take in their lives, but I hope they figure out that somewhere along the line the abundance they seek starts deep within. In the end, it's SMART to remember that the path to real abundance is as Lao Tzu says, "When you realize there is nothing lacking, the whole world belongs to you."

Chapter Eighteen

7 Pitfalls To Avoid When Rightsizing Your Home

"A house is no home unless it contains food and fire for the mind as well as for the body." ~Margaret Fuller

A friend of mine is currently in the midst of selling her long-time family home and moving. Yet while I believe she "gets" the many benefits of rightsizing, I can tell after talking with her that several issues keep popping up that make her hesitant. That's completely normal, because in many ways, rightsizing is contrary to what most of us have been taught. The good news is that once you know what to keep in mind, rightsizing not only becomes the easiest choice, it is also the one that leads to the greatest benefits.

What do we need to remember when it's time to make a move?

1) Don't rush to buy a home. This is particularly difficult if you've owned a home for as long as you can remember. It feels strange to rent because so many of us have identified and felt proud of ourselves as homeowners for so many years. However, the less a person has moved in the past, the more likely it is he or she will stay in their next home for many years, and maybe the rest of his or her life. That's why it is so important to take things slowly.

It is also likely that if you are selling a home and have a deadline to move it will seem very practical to only move one time—rather than live somewhere temporarily and then move again. Unfortunately, what usually happens is that you rush and then end up settling on a new home just so you don't have to move again. If you remember that the next home you buy might be your forever home, it makes sense to proceed as carefully as possible.

Besides, as a person who has moved over 16 times during my marriage, has owned dozens of properties, and who has been a real estate broker for over 30 years, I can assure you that taking things slowly is likely one of the best things you can do. A big reality is that the home of your dreams might not even be on the market today, but if you wait several months it could be right around the corner.

So what can you do? One choice is to spend a great deal of time looking before you ever put your home on the market to sell. Another option is to rent for a while. Temporary housing is also available that comes furnished allowing you to put most of your possessions in storage. The last time Thom and I moved, we sold most of our furniture, put the rest in storage, and then stayed in a friend's vacant second home for eight months while we shopped. Eventually, we found the right and perfect home and still live here five years later.

2) Weigh the benefits of renting vs. buying. Most of us in the baby boomer age category were raised believing that owning a home was equivalent to the American Dream. But what we may not have considered is that oftentimes the care, maintenance and unexpected costs of a home can make it more like the American Nightmare for some. The cost of ownership is easily about 25% higher, or more, than what most of us calculate. Renting can be the right choice if you aren't 100% sure of the home (or the location), if you can rent for less than you can own, or if your future is fuzzy and you don't know where it will lead.

3) Avoid buying a home as an investment. The best-selling book *THE MILLIONAIRE NEXT DOOR,* clearly explains that a home with a mortgage is a long-term liability. It COSTS YOU to live there. On the other hand, an investment GENERATES income. And although some people have made money in the past on a home they bought many years ago, a larger portion of the population lost money and even lost their homes when the economy tanked.

Besides, anyone who traditionally lives in a home for a long, long time should never consider what the home will be worth in the future. If this is your forever home, does it really matter what it's worth? Instead, focus on what it costs to live there and the benefits it provides.

4) Don't buy a home or anything you can't easily afford. One of the greatest benefits of rightsizing is making the conscious choice to buy only what you can easily afford—

especially a home. In fact, when Thom and I decided to go debt-free it was the best thing we did for our lifestyle. Even though we could have gotten another loan on a bigger house, we chose to compromise on a more compact dwelling in a neighborhood that fit our budget. In the end, we were able to obtain all the qualities in a home we desired making it the right and perfect place for us. Better to have freedom and peace of mind rather than extra square footage. We have not regretted our decision for a second in the last five years.

5) Don't buy a home to store your "stuff." One of the most common dilemmas I hear from people wanting to rightsize is that they don't know what to do with all their "stuff." Unfortunately, some buy a bigger house just because they can't let go of everything they've collected in life. I strongly recommend that you decide whether your future and your happiness require that stuff—and then act accordingly. But please, please don't buy a home just so you don't have to face what letting go of it really means.

6) Don't buy a house for your grandchildren. This is another pitfall I've seen grandparents fall into here in La Quinta, CA where I live. Because it is a desert community and swimming is popular, I know several grandparents who admitted they bought a bigger house with a swimming pool to entice the kids and grandkids to visit. Of course when family members do visit, they love the house and grandma and grandpa are happy. Sadly, those visits seldom meet expectations. Clearly that's an expensive gamble just for infrequent possibilities. Instead, why not just rent a vacation home with a pool, if or when you can actually get a date with your family, and save yourself a tremendous expense?

7) Don't buy where you've always lived just because you're afraid to try somewhere new. I get it. Some people are worried that if they move away from their family or existing friends they will be lonely. However, if your heart has always craved living somewhere different like near a beach, mountain, desert, city, country, or anything else different, what better time to try? Why not just rent for a while? Try different places. And don't think you have to move to another country either. By doing some research, you just might find a place that is far less expensive to live but offers you dozens of benefits you can't get where you are. And yes, your family/friends will visit you there too. Then again, you might be so busy and having so much fun you won't have that much time to miss them.

Bonus Tip: Stop caring about what other people think of the home you decide to choose. If the new property meets your needs on as many levels as possible, then you've rightsized your home and that is what really matters. After all, isn't your happiness and peace of mind more important than those who would judge you based on the price, size, location, or amenities of your home?

Remember, rightsizing is never about sacrificing. It is always about finding a place to live where you can be free to experience the life you've always wanted to live. Sure it takes some conscious deliberation and honest self-discovery, but the benefits will be more than you can imagine. By avoiding these pitfalls, the SMART choice is always to rightsize.

Final Thoughts—Enjoy The Journey

"Tell me, what is it you plan to do with your one precious life?"
~Mary Oliver

Hopefully after reading all my thoughts and examples of how to rightsize your life you've already started the process on your own. After all, rightsizing requires action! But if you've found yourself hesitating at all, I would like to leave you with three things I truly hope you remember after reading this book.

First of all, I want you to keep in mind that no rulebook exists on how to rightsize your life—including your retirement when the time comes. As I've said repeatedly, rightsizing is as individual as you are. While it might be easier to look at how others are doing it, and even to admire what others have created, unless your rightsized life fits your needs, dreams and requirements it won't be sustainable. Whittling away at things, distractions, ideas and pursuits that no longer serve you, and focusing in on what really works for you is the key. Let's never be intimidated or persuaded into believing there is only one right way to rightsize.

Secondly, I'd like to remind all of us that even though I believe rightsizing is a brilliant way to design your life, it will never be perfect and you'll never get it done. That's because as life changes, as we change, our hopes, dreams and desires for a rightsized life will change as well. It really doesn't matter if you are ready for retirement or just getting started in life. We can all begin right where we are. Besides, sometimes like the story of the Mexican man in his village, we find that after all our searching we are back where we started. That's perfectly good as long as the awareness of it eventually leads to fulfillment and happiness for our families and ourselves.

Finally, I believe it is very important for us all to remember that the beauty of rightsizing is that it is never a sacrifice. Sure, there are tradeoffs and sometimes we have to make some difficult decisions in order to carve out a life that works on many levels. But rather than seeing that experience as a sacrifice, I tend to believe it is just part of a journey that helps us be the very best each of us can be.

Rightsizing is the ultimate journey to find what matters to each of us, both inside ourselves and then in our homes, our community and the world we inhabit. Regardless of our ages or our circumstances, the process is available to us all. It is finding and creating a special place in our existence where we are most empowered to share our lives, our loves and our meaning with all we encounter. No matter where you are now, rightsizing is a journey to a more fulfilled life. Enjoy the ride!

ABOUT THE AUTHOR

Kathy Gottberg has authored hundreds of newsletters, articles, blog posts and four books during the last twenty-five years. Her insatiable curiosity continually leads her imagination, along with her writing, in all sorts of diverse and interesting directions. That's why she has proudly authored three works of nonfiction and one novel. Her current passion is writing and blogging at SMART Living 365.com where she explores practical ideas and experiences that lead to happiness, peace and well-being for all.

Kathy and her husband Thom have been partners in life and love for the last 38 years. They, and their dog Kloe, live in La Quinta, CA.

Contact The Author Online

To find current work and projects by Kathy Gottberg go to:

http://kathygottberg.com

http://smartliving365.com

Social Media Contacts:

Twitter: http://twitter.com/gottgreen

Facebook: http://www.facebook.com/SMARTLiving365